CHARLES AND DIANA

One of the greatest love stories of the century began with a telephone call to a flat shared by four bachelor girls near Buckingham Palace, inviting Lady Diana Spencer to be a week-end guest at Balmoral. Three days later she and Prince Charles knew that something very special had begun.

From that moment on Prince Charles and the girl who will be his future Queen could not bear to be apart from each other. He had his royal duties to carry out, but, whenever possible, he would speed to be with Diana. Six months were to pass before they officially announced this love to the world. A time in which the most eligible bachelor in the world thought carefully before making up his mind. Yes, Diana would be his Princess . . .

JANICE DUNLOP is a name well known to readers of newspapers and magazines in Britain and Europe, particularly concerning the activities of the Royal Family at home and abroad.

Charles and Diana

A Royal Romance

Janice Dunlop

CORONET BOOKS
Hodder and Stoughton

Copyright © Lock Associes 1981

First published 1981 in Coronet Books

British Library C.I.P.

Dunlop, Janice
Charles and Diana.
1. Charles, *Prince of Wales*
2. Spencer, *Lady* Diana
I. Title
941.085'8'0924   DA591.A33

ISBN 0-340-27274-0

Printed and bound in Great Britain for
Hodder and Stoughton Paperbacks, a
division of Hodder and Stoughton Ltd.,
Mill Road, Dunton Green, Sevenoaks,
Kent (Editorial Office: 47 Bedford
Square, London, WC1 3DP) by
Richard Clay (The Chaucer Press) Ltd.,
Bungay, Suffolk. Photoset by
Rowland Phototypesetting Ltd.,
Bury St Edmunds, Suffolk.

CONTENTS

5

ILLUSTRATIONS

An official engagement picture (1)
Golden wedding anniversary of Lady Diana's grandparents, with Lady Diana as a little girl (*front centre*) (2)
Lady Diana as a bridesmaid at her eldest sister's wedding (1)
Prince Charles in a play at Cambridge University during his student days (3)
Prince Charles at Cambridge, 1968 (3)
Prince Charles on a command course at Lympstone, Devon, November 1974 (3)
Prince Charles (bearded) with Prince Andrew and Captain Mark Phillips at Badminton (3)
Members of Lady Diana's family at a wedding (1)
Lady Diana's father, Earl Spencer, in the grounds of Althorp, the family home (1)
Mrs. Frances Shand-Kydd at home (mother of Lady Diana) (1)
The outside of Highgrove House, Prince Charles' home in the Cotswolds, 1980 (1)
The yellow bedroom at Highgrove House (1)
Lady Diana sitting alone in the grounds of the kindergarten, 1980 (1)
Lady Diana pushing a pram when working at the Young England kindergarten, 1980 (2)

Lady Diana with two of her charges at the kindergarten, September 1980 (1)

Prince Charles with Lady Diana and the Queen Mother in the paddock at Sandown Park, March 13th, 1981 (1)

Lady Diana at Sandown races to watch Prince Charles ride in the Military Gold Cup (3)

Lady Diana before the engagement, 1981 (2)

Lady Diana and Prince Charles at their first public function together, attending a concert at Goldsmith Hall, London, 1981 (3)

An official engagement picture (1)

(1) Press Association
(2) Photographers International
(3) Serge Lemoine

Chapter One

A TELEPHONE RINGS

The shrill sound of the telephone bell cut across the girlish clamour in the mansion block first floor flat over-looking Old Brompton Road, a pleasant enough but un-distinguished shopping street placed less than two miles from the tourist sights of Buckingham Palace and a convenient ten minutes brisk walk from Knightsbridge and the world famous top people's store, Harrods. Phone calls always caused excitement at the flat in Coleherne Court. For, when girls leave home for the first time to share a flat together in a big city the telephone becomes their link to the outside world full of single men: the invitations to dinner, to week-ends in the country, the prospect of love, romance, even marriage.

In this crowded three-bedroomed flat shared by four girls, all in their late teens or early twenties the phone was constantly in use, particularly in the evenings. It had been installed in the hall so that each of the girls, who had been living together for just over a year, would have some degree of privacy for their quiet chats and whispered confidences. Not that there were any secrets between these four who had left home to find excitement in London. They shared one another's happiness and interest over new boyfriends and the tears and brief despair over shattered romances. But most of all their

9

small world rang with the sound of the laughter they shared.

Dark haired Virginia Pitman was the first to reach the phone. Aged twenty-one, she was the most ebullient and extrovert of the 'famous four', a name coined from the Enid Blyton stories they had all read as children. After listening there was an uncharacteristic frown across her forehead as she put the receiver down and went into the living-room. It was cluttered, but considering the close proximity of four young women, reasonably tidy: in this flat there was a rota and all the girls had their housekeeping jobs to do. "Diana, it's for you," Virginia told the organiser of the rota, a blonde girl in jeans and sweater who owned the flat. "It's some man who says he is from Buckingham Palace. It must be his idea of a joke."

The blonde strode across to the phone. "Yes, this is Diana Spencer." She listened for about a minute with only the occasional "yes" and "I understand", but when she put the phone back on the hook she was flushed with excitement. The news she had to tell Virginia and her two other flatmates Ann Bolton and Carolyn Pride made all the girls shriek with excitement, because the girl whom the others so jokingly called the "landlady" had been invited to spend the week-end at Balmoral, the Scottish castle of the British Royal Family. Ann, Virginia and Carolyn, all very well brought up young ladies from the top drawer of English society did not need to be told who or what Balmoral was. All realised what such an invitation meant in the complex pecking order of the English upper classes.

Two days later Diana was standing in a queue at Heathrow. The name on her ticket just read Miss D. Spencer and the passenger list for the British Airways

10

flight gave no clues to the small knot of keen eyed, rather scruffily dressed men waiting at the entrance to the departure gate in the ultra modern number one terminal building. The date was 5 September, 1980 and 19-year-old Diana, a kindergarten teacher, fresh out of school herself, was off on a rendezvous which would change the life of this girl who was born a lady but was destined to become a princess and one day a queen. The keen-eyed men at the gate were journalists and their eyes flickered across the thick, well brushed tresses of the girl who clutched her ticket and a small brown leather overnight bag.

"No, that's not her," said burly Ray Watts, an experienced old hand at spotting the one face among the thousands who flood through Heathrow every day. This group of five men, one other reporter, Ray and three photographers, their Nikons and flash guns always at the ready, were looking for one blonde in particular. Ray clutched a newspaper clipping with a creased picture of a stunningly beautiful woman, who seemed much more sophisticated and glamorous than the Miss D. Spencer he had ignored in the queue. The pressmen were eager for a piece for the morning paper gossip columns, a lucrative bit of scandal about the latest episode in the love life of the 31-year-old bachelor heir to the English throne.

The same passenger list which bore the name D. Spencer also carried a D. Sheffield, a significant name and destination on that cool September afternoon towards the end of a wet and miserable summer. The mass-market daily papers had all reported that the ups and downs of the dashing Prince Charming's much-reported love life had reached a low ebb, so it was likely that an old friend would be invited to brighten up the

11

week-end. The name Sheffield looked like a winner. Until now, Davina Sheffield had easily been the prettiest of the Prince's collection of lovely women companions. It was well known that although their twelve month romance had ended some eighteen months previously, the two had kept in touch. So the Heathrow press crew ignored the unknown Miss D. Spencer as she boarded the British Airways Trident jet for the flight to Aberdeen. The events of the forthcoming week-end would make them curse with frustration when they realised what they had missed. But Diana herself would have been surprised if they had taken her photograph because as far as she was concerned she had been invited to Balmoral by Queen Elizabeth II for a friendly, informal family week-end. She didn't know who had prompted the invitation because he wanted to meet again the lovely schoolgirl whom he was later to tell the world he only remembered as "a splendid girl, so full of fun". Yet neither Prince Charles nor Diana could have dreamed that less than twenty-four hours later they would both suddenly realise they were in love . . . a love which sparked off a whirlwind courtship and which ended with a marriage proposal just six months later over a candlelit supper at Buckingham Palace.

The most eligible bachelor in the world would fall helplessly in love with an attractive, blue-eyed teenager, hardly out of school and twelve years his junior. Diana was born with a title, a real life Lady with a position of privilege, but nevertheless a child of our times, her family broken up by divorce. Overnight, with the stroke of a pen, she would become a member of the Royal Family and be called Princess of Wales, Countess of Chester, Duchess of Cornwall, Duchess of Rothesay, Countess of Garrick and Baroness Renfrew. She would inherit enormous wealth and power and one day be crowned Queen of England.

Diana and Charles' love story would become the romance of the century.

It was dark when the Trident touched down at Dyce, Aberdeen's airport, once a sleepy terminal with just a couple of flights a day but now grown to handle the traffic generated by the North Sea oil finds. Lady Diana joined the 100 or so other passengers, mostly workers heading back for another hard two-month spell on the rigs battered by endless northern gales or dark-suited businessmen with fat briefcases off to clinch another deal involving Britain's substantial 'black gold' undersea discoveries. Just as at Heathrow 514 miles away, Dyce Airport had its passenger-watchers too: two Scottish photographers from the *Daily Express* and the *Daily Mail*. They also missed the blonde Lady Diana. In her below-knee-length fashionable dark grey skirt and light blue windcheater she looked just like any of the local girls, dressed against what passed for summer this far north. That afternoon it had rained in Aberdeen, nothing unusual for Scotland where mist and cloud was part of the country's attractions.

The bracing climate had been the delight of generations of hardy Royals who had made Royal Deeside into their traditional summer retreat. The present Royal Family carried on the tradition begun by Queen Victoria of enjoying the exhilaration of early morning horseback gallops across heather-covered moorland, grouse shoots and icy fishing expeditions for the silver salmon which leap from the fast flowing waters of the Dee.

One airport-worker, however, blending in among the

locals in green waterproof anorak, tweed suit and sensible walking shoes, spotted Diana. This man was in his late twenties, well spoken, quiet and unassuming. Under his jacket he wore a fully loaded revolver in a soft leather holster. He was one of the thirty or so Royal detectives, hand-picked by Scotland Yard to protect the top ten members of the Royal Family. The gun guard round the Royals, particularly Prince Charles, had in the past always been very low key. But the assassination in the previous year of the Prince's uncle, Lord Louis Mountbatten, by the Irish Republican Army had changed all that. Now all the Royals and even their guests were protected by these young Scotland Yard men, rather like the American Secret Service agents who guard their President.

The young man approached Lady Diana, having been briefed by Buckingham Palace to expect her. He led her to a green Range Rover parked in a no-waiting area at the side of the airport terminal building. She sat in the front passenger seat for the drive out westwards along the twisting A93 which runs from Aberdeen through the beautiful forest of Glentanar to the River Dee and the purple heather-covered hills surrounding the market town of Ballater and the Castle of Balmoral. With a wave to the policeman sitting guard in the gatehouse entrance to the castle, Diana's driver swept up to the main door of the ancient turretted building.

That night the teenager dined with the Queen, Prince Philip, the Queen Mother and the youngest Prince, Edward, then sixteen-years-old and still at Gordonstoun School in Scotland. They sat in Balmoral's state dining room hung with stained and torn flags from battle victories long since past, and were served the plain food favoured by the Royal Family, roast meat and vegetables, by liveried footmen in scarlet jackets carrying silver salvers. Diana, of course, knew everyone there and felt completely at ease in the Royal company. But her attention was on the Prince who sat opposite her. Diana had met Charles earlier that summer: once at Balmoral when she went there to help her sister Jane, married to Robert Fellowes the Queen's assistant private secretary, with Jane's first baby, and before that at a glittering ball at the Duke of Richmond's Goodwood House during the Goodwood race meeting. At Goodwood the Prince began to notice for the first time how the shy, vulnerable adolescent had blossomed into full womanhood. He had asked her to dance. They waltzed together beautifully, but friends took little notice.

In July the Prince had discovered Diana's wicked sense of humour, so much like his own. He remembered how she had been part of a large party aboard the Royal Yacht *Britannia* for the Cowes Regatta on the Isle of Wight and how she ducked him in the icy waters of the Solent by tipping over the mast of his wind surfer. There have been few girls who could get away with such impishness. At Balmoral in July they had laughed again over the prank. It was the laughter they shared which prompted the Prince to suggest to the Queen that Diana would make a fine September guest.

The talk at dinner was of the salmon leaping in the ten miles of River Dee owned by the Royal Family. Prince Charles suggested an early morning fishing expedition the next morning and the now not-so-shy Diana was delighted. She is a fresh and deceptively unsophisticated girl who shares all the delights of the rugged outdoor life favoured by the Prince. He had been nicknamed 'Action man' because of his hunting, shooting, riding, diving, skiing and racing pastimes. Fortunately, she had been brought up in the country and a day's fishing in icy waters held no horrors for her. The next morning after breakfast, the couple set off in the green Range Rover with the Prince's favourite gun dog, Harvey, a golden labrador, with a set of fishing rods attached to the side of the vehicle in a special rack.

The spot the Prince picked was one of the best fishing spots on the Dee, near a bend in the river five miles from Balmoral. Here the crystal clear water cascades over hundreds of small granite rocks. It is a place where he landed many prize fish and a spot favoured by another keen Royal angler, his grandmother the Queen Mother. At the grand age of eighty she still came down to these waters to cast her line. But on this overcast, slightly damp and chilly Saturday morning the couple had the river bank to themselves. Although one side of the bank was exclusively Royal the other was open to anyone with enough money to afford the pricey fishing permits. There was not even a detective lurking nearby because the Prince was thought to be perfectly safe inside the thousands of acres of private Balmoral estate

This was the first time Diana and Charles had ever been completely alone together and what went on or was discussed during the next two hours must forever remain a secret between the two of them. But this is the moment the relationship took off, the moment Prince Charles stopped thinking of Diana as a schoolgirl who was 'full of fun'. The discovery of one another, interspersed as always with the laughter from the sense of fun they both share, was the stepping off point towards love and marriage. Their platonic friendship changed forever from that morning: from that day on the Prince, who always had a keen eye for a pretty girl, had eyes for no one else.

But as they chatted and laughed, the Prince in thigh high rubber waders out in the current and Lady Diana sitting on the bank beside a fir tree, the privacy of their two snatched hours away from the world was rudely shattered. The Prince suddenly strode back to the bank, an angry look on his face. He reached for a pair of binoculars from the back of the Range Rover and turned them on the opposite bank. Thirty yards across the river a photographer was focussing a long range lens. It is not clear whether the Prince, wary as a hunted deer of lone cameramen, gave the instruction or whether it was the lady herself who decided with remarkable speed to ruin a scoop for the photographer. Safely hidden behind the nearest tree Lady Diana fished in her pocket for a powder compact and using the mirror in its lid she peered furtively out from her hiding place. Photographer Ken Lennox was rewarded with a smudgy print of an angry looking Prince and the back of a lady in a headscarf peering into her make-up mirror. On Monday morning the photograph was splashed across the pages of the national newspaper who employed Lennox. It was a look into the future for Diana, a taste of what she must expect, a fate suffered by many pretty girls in the past who have been seen with the Prince. Fleet Street and the rest of the world's press, hungry for romance stories about the bachelor heir to the throne, would never leave her alone now. Her cover was broken before the romance had even started. The seeds of romance sown that morning in those two stolen hours together would change the lives of both these young people.

That afternoon, with the Queen and Prince Philip, the Prince attended the Highland Games at nearby Braemar dressed in his ceremonial tartan kilt and tweed jacket. There was no sign of the mysterious lady on the river

17

bank, much to the annoyance of a large posse of reporters and photographers. On Sunday night Lady Diana was driven back to Dyce Airport but by then her identity had been discovered by the newsmen. From Heathrow, Diana took a taxi back to Coleherne Court and the three flatmates who were desperate to know all about the week-end at Balmoral. A phone call just before midnight pushed the excitement to fever pitch. Prince Charles was calling from his room at Balmoral more than 500 miles away. He and Diana talked for an hour and a further date was made for later that month when the Prince returned from Scotland.

At 8.30 the next morning Diana drove across London to the kindergarten in Pimlico, near Victoria, where she had been working for the last fourteen months, helping to look after fifty infants, four days a week. She didn't know it then but it was the last time she would be able to take that twenty minute drive in peace before the eyes of the world were turned on her. When she arrived back at her flat at teatime the first photographer was waiting to snap her; for the next six months there would not be one day when she would be able to return home without finding a cameraman lurking somewhere. On Tuesday with the kindergarten also under siege by about ten journalists, she agreed to pose with two of her charges in the hope, vain as it happened, that they would agree to leave her alone. But the lady made a slip, or rather forgot her slip and the ensuing photo session became an incident which left Diana red-faced with embarrassment.

That Tuesday had begun warm with bright sunshine and Diana had put on a thin skirt bought earlier in the summer from Liberty's the Regent Street store, popular with young ladies of her background. The flowery cotton print looked very cool and fresh. The playground of the

18

Young England kindergarten behind a church in St. George's Square, Pimlico, was shaded by several flowering cherry trees and the photographers asked her to move out of the shadow to get the sun behind her to enhance her fair skin and blonde hair. It is an old cameraman's trick to get a sort of halo effect, very flattering in black and white. Diana walked across the playground with two four-year-old children and picked up one child to pose shyly, standing where the men had asked her. What she didn't realise, as the battery-operated motor drives whirred on, was that through the lens of their expensive cameras the delighted photographers were getting a real eyefull. The sun shining through the thin material revealed very fine legs and the shots, when they appeared less than two hours later in the first editions of the London evening papers, made the lady blush a deep beetroot red. "Oh my God," she exclaimed to the other teachers. "I've never been so embarrassed in all my life." But the next day when the Prince made his second call to her flat after seeing the same photos in the morning papers they laughed together as he made jokes about the strong, well-shaped limbs which the world had seen for itself.

Laughter was an ingredient which had been missing from the Prince's private life for more than two months. The Prince, who admits to being a romantic, falling easily but usually very briefly, in love, had been a very lonely young man before the discoveries of the Balmoral weekend. The precious winter he had met another blonde who was to have a profound effect on his life. Freckle-faced millionaire's daughter, Anna Wallace, was the most independent and fiery girl the Prince had ever known well. The slim-waisted, 25-year-old woman was considered by many to be one of the most attractive of his companions. Their friendship began after a chance meeting at a winter weekend hunting party.

As a future bride her background was perfect. Her extremely wealthy father, Hamish Wallace, owned homes and estates in England and Scotland and a house in fashionable Charles Street, Mayfair, just behind the Hilton Hotel. The only thing in her disfavour were her former relationships. Charles knew all about the problems of old boyfriends. Davina Sheffield too had a previous boyfriend before the Prince, who had come forward to reveal all to the millions of readers of a popular Sunday newspaper. The revelations greatly embarrassed the Prince. But in the winter and spring of 1980 Charles pursued the lovely Anna, a girl who looked for excitement in life. She spent several week-ends with him as a guest at the homes of several of his trusted friends and he made regular visits to her small flat just off Sloane Square, Chelsea, ironically less than a mile from the flat he would never visit, Lady Diana's home at Coleherne Court. But Anna, although flattered by the Prince's attentions, was not a girl who would or could easily fall in love with the Royal lifestyle. She objected to the way she had to be picked up by detectives and driven for secret and furtive rendezvous with the Prince. The wooing of any girl by a prince is bound to be shrouded in secrecy but Anna wanted none of this.

Charles believed he was in love with the lovely Anna and even told one of his male friends that he wanted to marry her, but it was Anna herself who settled the problem. She had become sick and tired of her undercover lifestyle and when one night in June at a ball given by his old friend Lord Vestey the Prince danced all night with other girls, leaving Anna alone, her emerald green eyes flashed with anger. When he did ask her to dance, the couple rowed and other dancers heard Anna exclaim, "You've left me alone all night, now you will have to do without me." She drove home alone that night and although the telephone calls kept coming through to her from Buckingham Palace she never saw the Prince again. Two months later, on 21 August in the pages of The *Times*, right next to the official Court Circular (where Charles couldn't fail to see it), Anna announced her forthcoming marriage to another man, Johnny, the younger brother of an English Peer, Lord Hesketh. It was a fine match for Anna.

Through the months of July and August the Prince had become a lonely man. He carried out his scores of public engagements with style as always, giving no sign of personal feelings, but he still spent many hours alone in his small apartment inside Buckingham Palace. Strangely enough during all this period the thought of marriage must have been uppermost in his mind. Suddenly he decided to go house hunting. He might not have a bride but he would have a home. The management of the Duchy of Cornwall, which was responsible for the thousands of acres of prime land in the lovely green counties of Gloucestershire, Wiltshire and Devon owned by the Prince as part of his birthright, received an instruction from Buckingham Palace, to look out for a suitable large country home with enough style to make it fit for a prince. A few days later, clutching the brochure from a real estate agent, Prince Charles turned his midnight blue Ford Granada off the A433, through a set of rusting wrought-iron gates, and crunched his way up a half-mile gravel drive. He turned to the man at his side, a representative of Humberts, a firm of auctioneers: "This looks interesting," he said.

Less than an hour later after wandering through the

distinguished Georgian house, its four beautifully appointed reception rooms, nine bedrooms, six bathrooms and having slipped on some green rubber boots to tramp round some of the 346 acres of rich arable farmland, the Prince had made up his mind. "I'll have it," he said simply and the Highgrove Estate, in the tiny village of Doughton near the market town of Tetbury, in the wooded Gloucestershire countryside and less than 100 miles from London, became Royal property for the princely sum of £800,000. But before the deal was finally struck one lady was asked to give her view. Two weeks after their rediscovery of one other on the banks of the River Dee, the Prince invited Lady Diana to see Highgrove for herself. He wanted a woman's view of what he considered was his dream home. She would never have even dreamed that one day Highgrove would be the house they would share as man and wife, but perhaps somewhere, even then, the Prince had realised how perfect Diana was for him and needed her opinion of what he considered a rare find in the English countryside.

Diana drove up to the imposing white painted double front door which is flanked by a fine colonnaded porch. Charles was waiting in the magnificent oak-floored main hall beside an impressive marble fireplace. Behind him was a view to the west through a bay window with french doors to the formal garden beyond. Alone together they strolled into the drawing room with its fitted window seats and Irish marble fireplace and into the library with its fitted bookshelves on two walls. From then on the tour of the rooms downstairs seemed endless. The dining room, the billiard room, butler's pantry, kitchen with stone flagged floor and an old fashioned solid fuel cooker. By Diana's standards Highgrove, built in 1763 but later substantially refurbished, is a small house. Her

22

father's huge red brick Elizabethan manor, Althorp, 160 miles further north near the industrial city of Northampton, was far grander. Althorp, containing one of the finest private art collections in Europe was an enormous property, so big that members of the public could be taken on guided tours without any embarrassment or disruption to normal life for the Spencer family living in just one wing. Highgrove would neatly fit into the area covered by staff flats and outbuildings at Althorp.

But Diana was delighted with Highgrove and hurried up the wide easy tread staircase into the master bedroom, known at that time by the present owners, Mr. Maurice Macmillan, a Conservative member of Parliament, and son of the former Premier, as the Yellow Room. Then the couple went down the corridor to what could become the most important area in the house . . . the spot which one day soon may become the focus of world attention. A fully self-contained nursery wing. Lady Diana looked at the nineteen by fifteen foot nursery itself complete with open fireplace and toy cupboard before moving on to see the bedrooms intended for a nanny and her maid; two small, plainly-fitted rooms sharing one bathroom. The lady was thrilled with Highgrove and later that year, after the news of her engagement, she would tell her friends: "It's perfect, I just couldn't wish for a nicer house."

Chapter Two

MEETINGS AND SEPARATIONS

On week-ends throughout the autumn and winter Diana
would return again and again to Highgrove which by
then had been stripped of all furniture. The Prince
adored the house and its beautiful parkland which includes a superbly maintained formal garden dominated
by a magnificent cedar of Lebanon. Cut leaf beech and
tulip trees are set among the carefully clipped lawns and
well pruned rose beds. The Royal decorator, David
Hicks, who had helped design many Royal households,
was instructed to take a look at Highgrove and submit a
basic plan. But he didn't need anybody else to tell him
about the reorganisation of the stable block, a brick and
slate building fifty yards from the main house, which
would become home for the Prince's string of polo
ponies, his hunters and his beloved racehorse Allibar, a
magnificent eleven-year-old gelding which he had
bought the previous year. Apart from the fact that he
adored Highgrove, the house's situation in Gloucestershire held other interests for him. He was always in the
area during the winter months, hunting with the
Beaufort pack dressed in his navy and scarlet riding
jacket galloping behind a pack of baying hounds. The
Prince of Wales, like many of his ancestors, adores to ride

across ploughed fields and over briar hedges after the scent of a fox.

There was also another reason for buying Highgrove. Just five miles away across woods and a stream, lived his sister Princess Anne, her husband Captain Mark Phillips, recently retired army officer turned gentleman farmer and show jumper, and their infant son Peter. Charles had always been very close to his sister and since they moved from London to live at Gatcombe Park, a country estate not unlike Highgrove, he had been a frequent visitor. Living so close would be very convenient for them both.

The romance of the decade had started but it would be a strange sort of courtship for the twentieth century. The wooing of Lady Diana Spencer would not be all champagne and roses, candlelight suppers or country house parties. There would be tears and subterfuge, despair and loneliness. The tears would be shed by Lady Diana, overwhelmed more than once by the pressure she faced. The subterfuge and despair would be shared by them both as they tried to escape the world's curiosity with pre-arranged phone calls, long drives and furtive meetings at the homes of mutual, trusted friends. They would be in love but never be seen in public together throughout their courtship, never hold hands in case anyone was watching. Never relax completely with each other, existing only from one snatched rendezvous to the next. They would be forced to act as if their relationship were somehow dirty, hiding, forever suspicious, never knowing whom to trust. The loneliness would be shared by them both. She in her Coleherne Court flat and he in the empty rooms of Highgrove or in his private quarters at Buckingham Palace.

But it was still September, the romance had only just

begun and their problems hadn't even started yet. Through October the couple met whenever they could with a set arrangement of pre-timed phone calls, long late night drives and false trails designed to throw off the watching press. The world had already realised that this wasn't just another of "Charlie's darlings" as the popular press put it. Diana was obviously someone special. In-depth assessments of her began to appear even in the more respectable British newspapers. Diana was being photographed constantly wherever she went. Sensing a winner at last, the men and women journalists from Europe and North America were moving in on the flat at Coleherne Court. A picture of Lady Diana just getting out of her car would get front page treatment: none of Charles' past girlfriends had ever earned such attention.

Diana tried to carry on as usual, dancing with the children who called her "Miss Diana" at the kindergarten: she even found time late in the afternoon for two days of her week to care for a young handicapped child, spending several hours at a flat in exclusive Eaton Square, Belgravia. The child's name was Patrick and Diana became quite dedicated to him and was upset when he returned to America with his parents. The kindergarten and her hours with Patrick revealed her love for children. The infants she helped to care for there were only at pram or pushchair age, and her work was as a sort of nanny. She may not have realised that she was preparing for marriage and motherhood in a loving and practical way.

Diana's week-ends, wherever possible, were spent with the Prince. He was constantly on the phone to her flat and her flatmates, who came to be christened the 'Trinian belles' after a famous series of British films on hilarious schoolgirl life, were drawn into the royal romance too. Throughout the six months all three girls were constantly pressurised by reporters desperate to get any information on Charles or Diana, but none ever revealed a thing. As Carolyn, who was at school with Lady Diana said after the news of the engagement, "It wasn't difficult to keep it secret; we never dreamed of telling anyone. We have been very discreet." Secrecy was the name of the game played by the couple that month. Diana was never seen with him in public although on a number of occasions she had managed to be nearby as he went hunting and shooting. She was in the grandstand at Ludlow racecourse in Shropshire as the Prince, mounted on Allibar, engaged in his latest hobby, horse racing, the sport of kings. She cheered him and screamed with excitement as he was narrowly beaten into second place. But she sneaked away from the course alone to meet him later in the evening to celebrate his near victory over a champagne dinner at the home of one of the Prince's friends.

Even his thirty-second birthday on 14 November had to be celebrated in secrecy. The Prince had gone to another of the Royal Family's country homes, Sandringham, a beautiful but wild and windswept country estate on Britain's east coast in the county of Norfolk. The estate was under siege by a small army of pressmen. Eventually Diana had to say her 'happy birthdays' over the telephone and the presents she had bought in Knightsbridge, including two sensible plain white shirts from Harrods had to wait until the press interest had waned. Buying presents for the man who has everything is not easy, neither is being unable to join his birthday party.

In the middle of November came the first taste of the real loneliness and despair she would experience in her new role and with their first real separation came the first tears. She had driven down to Highgrove to spend Saturday night, virtually camping out on the now stripped and bare boards looked after only by an elderly Irish couple who had worked for the Macmillans and had stayed on to manage the house for its new owner. The next morning the Prince had to say his first long 'goodbye' of their relationship. That evening he was flying from Heathrow airport to Delhi at the start of a well-planned royal tour of the Indian sub-continent. For three weeks they would be separated by 6,000 miles.

In her flat Diana sat with her flatmates in front of their colour TV to watch the Prince's ceremonial arrival at Delhi airport on the early evening news. On Tuesday night he telephoned her from the palace in the Indian capital which had been the home of the last Englishman to rule India's millions, the late Lord Louis Mountbatten, the man Prince Charles had called 'Uncle Dickie'. The telephone line from Delhi was terrible, the couple had to shout to make themselves understood, but his call made it obvious that he missed her already. During the next two weeks telephone calls would come in from all parts of India – from Bombay, Madras, Agra, Bangalore and Calcutta. Sometimes the phone in Coleherne Court rang in the early hours of the morning. India was five-and-a-half-hours ahead of London time and it was only late at night, after the daily round of receptions and dinners, that the Prince could get to a phone. Sometimes he took ages to get through: even the Prince of Wales, an honoured guest, did not get much in the way of priority from the ancient Indian telegram service. It was during one of these bad connections, with the line faltering and breaking up and with a strange echo effect making conversation virtually impossible that Diana burst into tears.

Diana had been bitterly upset by a story in one of Britain's papers alleging, totally without truth, that she had spent an illicit night of love with the Prince, before his departure for India, in the carriage of the Royal train parked on a railway siding in the West Country. Lady Diana had been nowhere near the train at the time. In fact on the night in question she had driven back to her flat after joining the Prince and the rest of the Royal Family at a belated birthday party for Princess Margaret, the Queen's younger sister, in the ballroom of the Ritz Hotel in Piccadilly. That night had been one of the happiest of their new friendship. Wearing a blue satin gown, her shoulders bare, Diana had danced all night with Charles and had enjoyed supper with her childhood chum Prince Andrew, then twenty, and one of his many girlfriends, a lovely model named Gemma Curry. Gemma was just nineteen and she and Diana found they had much in common.

The story had ruined Diana's memories of a wonderful fairytale evening. And she wept as she told Charles about the innuendo and gossip the story had spread. Her distress upset and angered the Prince who instructed his private secretary to demand an apology from the newspaper, an unprecedented move for the Royal Family. In any ordinary situation Diana could have sued for libel over such a tale but the Royal Family had never done such a thing: a court hearing would be unthinkable. In the event the Queen's Press Secretary, Mr. Michael Shea, wrote to the editor demanding an apology and even issued a copy of his letter to the rest of Fleet Street. Usually the Royal Family ignored wild stories written about their activities, so by his anger over Diana's tears the Prince had unwittingly revealed how much he cared for her. This chink in his armour did not go unnoticed by the small group of British journalists tailing him on his tour of schools, factories, farms and ancient temples throughout India. Amazingly, and most uncharacteristically, the Prince, who over the years had become something of an expert in hiding his private affairs from the press, revealed the first inkling of the strain teenage Diana had been under since the Balmoral week-end in September. Chatting about nothing in particular to a trio of British reporters at a reception in the British High Commission in Delhi the Prince, among all the small talk about the weather and the Indian poverty and way of life, suddenly started talking about the girl they all wanted to know about but didn't dare ask. "Diana's a very nice girl, you know," he said and quickly added: "All this has been something of a strain for her. At times it has reduced her to tears, but she has coped magnificently."

Then he told about some of the problems and worries running through his own mind about the girl he cared so much about. "You must not rush me," he told the amazed men from Fleet Street. "If I get it all wrong you will be the first to criticise me in a few years' time. It's all right for you chaps. You can live with a girl before you marry her, but I can't. I've got to get it right from the word go." It was a rare insight into the secret, very human dilemma which faced the heir to the throne. The problem facing Charles was, could Diana at the tender age of nineteen be that very special lady? She was obviously a charming, sweet girl – anyone could see that. But did she have enough – to use the words of Queen Victoria talking about Princess Alexandra, the future Princess of Wales in February 1881 – "to take the foremost position in the society of the greatest and richest capital in the world".

Britain was no longer the capital of the world, but the

safe and secure British monarchy was at a pinnacle of success. The crown was popular and much loved. Thousands had turned out that summer to sing "happy birthday" to the 80-year-old Queen Mother. It was a time of great faith in the Queen and Prince Philip, a time when the popularity of the Royal Family had reached a peak. The problem of whether or not Diana was the right girl bore down heavily on the shoulders of the heir as he finished off an exhausting Indian tour with a trip to the poverty and horror of the most overcrowded city on earth, Calcutta. The Prince, too well-trained to show emotion, came close to tears himself as he walked through the shaded top floor room at Lower Circular Road, in the heart of teeming Calcutta. Incense smoke drifted across dozens of tiny wooden cots crammed in lines. He was clearly moved when he saw Leela, a three-day-old girl who had been found barely alive, stuffed like garbage into a dustbin in the filthy slums which cover that impoverished city. He had discovered that nothing in the ordinary western response had equipped him to cope with the shock as Nobel prize winner, Mother Teresa, told him in a quiet matter of fact manner that if baby Leela had not been found in time by the nuns, the baby would have been eaten by the packs of wild dogs which roam the tin shacks and cardboard shelters, home of countless millions.

Later, slightly to the north of Kathmandu in Nepal, Prince Charles found himself alone at last, with time to think. He finally made up his mind to ask Diana to be his bride. He would not make the actual proposal for two more months, but trekking through the dramatic beauty of the Himalayas had given him precious time to work things out. He knew that the speculation and excitement would reach a climax the moment he stepped back on to

31

the tarmac at Heathrow. For three days he walked and camped below the permanent mountain snows. He wasn't completely alone, but then these days a Prince never is. But cosseted as he was by security men, porters, guides and his entourage of secretary, press officer and personal doctor, the Prince still found solitude, walking out in front on the trails which wound through beautiful green valleys and up into the sub-tropical foliage of foothills leading to the very roof of the world. Charles returned to civilisation near a small village called Pokhara on 12 December. Tanned and unshaven with a bright red frangipani blossom through the buttonhole of his khaki jacket, the Prince was in a delightfully relaxed mood after nearly four days of living rough in the mountains. Before driving off to a hot bath he said: "It was so wonderfully relaxing, I feel so well. It was marvellous to wake up in the morning, open the tent window and see the mountains framed like a picture. You could hear absolutely nothing . . . that silence." The Prince had obviously enjoyed the chance to get away from the world to think about what was to be the most important decision of his life.

From Pokhara he flew back to Kathmandu and dinner with his old friend, the King of Nepal, in the Royal Palace. His Majesty, King Birendra, is an Old Etonian public schoolboy who is three years older than Prince Charles and regarded by some of his subjects as the reincarnation of a Hindu God. To Charles the King was just an old friend. The next day he piloted his Andover from Kathmandu airport 3,000 miles to Bahrain, refuelling in Oman. It was difficult to fault the conduct of the Prince during the difficult, and sometimes controversial, Indian tour. He had been treated with suspicion when he arrived in Delhi, memories of British colonial rule were still there, but by the end of the tour he had won friends for Britain by his charm, compassion and diplomacy. At Bahrain the Prince joined 200 other passengers on an ordinary British Airways scheduled flight from the Seychelles, and finally touched down at Heathrow late in the evening of 14 December. Once home he realised immediately that the controversy over Lady Diana was just as strong. A huge possè of pressmen were waiting on the tarmac.

One excited photographer among the throng accidentally crashed into a litter bin as he backed down a corridor trying to photograph the immaculately dressed Prince. The good humour of the last few days vanished with the crash of the litter bin hitting the concrete. "Pick it up," he told the red-faced cameraman angrily. "Anyone would think there's a war going on." In an obvious bad mood he strode out to his waiting Ford. He took the wheel and drove away so fast that he almost stalled the engine. The Prince had received only a temporary reprieve from the controversy raging over his head about Lady Diana, but now he was back in the thick of it. He could not even get away from it in Buckingham Palace. When he arrived back at his small private apartment straight from Heathrow he was told the Queen wanted to see him. He could guess what she wanted to talk about.

Chapter Three

THE PRINCE MAKES HIS MOVE

The Queen had hardly ever mentioned his previous romances even when the facts were emblazoned across the morning papers. But this time the speculation over Lady Diana had grown to fever pitch and she had told one of the household, "Even I don't know what is happening." She had asked to see him on his return from Nepal because like any other mother, she was burning with curiosity to know if this was *the* girl at last. Her curiosity would have to wait a few more weeks. The next morning Charles was up early – he is by nature an early riser – out of bed most days by 6 a.m. at the latest. "I can't see the point in lying in bed, there's too much to do," he once said. He gathered his detective and armed Special Branch back-up team and sped off to the West Country to join an early morning hunt with the Beaufort. It would not be until Christmas that his mother would manage to pin him down about his intentions.

Dutifully from the age of twenty-one Prince Charles had done all the rounds and met all the right upper class available young ladies and never really taken to any of them. He had even travelled to Luxembourg, under conditions of great secrecy a few years previously to meet a real life Princess, Marie-Astrid, and discovered that they had little in common, especially religion. For Charles the whole idea of an arranged marriage was completely abhorrent. But even his father, Prince Philip had started telling him, jokingly at first and later, after the Prince's thirty-first birthday with much more seriousness: "You'd better hurry up, or there won't be anyone left." But the Prince had waited. He had always told his friends that he wanted to marry for love and now just a few days from Christmas 1980 he believed he had found it at last. In the next few weeks he would broach the subject of marriage with Diana herself, tentatively at first, without making a formal proposal, because Charles did have one further worry. What if Lady Diana should say "no"? He knew that she wouldn't just be making a decision to marry a man, she would be marrying into a way of life, a job, the task of helping Charles with the difficult problem of steering the monarchy into the twenty-first century. He would first hint at the idea of marriage to give her time to think. As he admitted after the news of their eventual engagement was announced, he wanted to give her the chance of telling him: "I can't bear the whole idea." About her acceptance he said: "I am frankly amazed that Diana is prepared to take me on."

It was just before Christmas when Charles and Diana met for their reunion and he chose the home of his old and well trusted friends, the Parker-Bowles, at Allington, a pretty little village near Chippenham, Wiltshire. Diana later told friends that Charles seemed "strangely stifled". But then that was only to be expected from a man whose mind contained such serious but happy thoughts. His actual words must, of course, remain a secret but from what had trickled through from Diana via her friends and family, the Prince put it in a sort of "If I were to ask you" way. He must have been rather taken aback when the lady giggled. She said later that she had immediately felt the absurdity of the situation and couldn't help giggling. The way the proposal was put didn't warrant an answer at that time and the Prince didn't expect one. But immediately and particularly over the Christmas holiday, wedding plans were discussed. Diana hadn't said "yes" yet. But it was still necessary to make plans. A Royal wedding requires incredibly complex forward planning. The traditional wedding organiser, the Duke of Norfolk, was asked to keep his engagement diary free from mid-April until 31 July. Heads of the Commonwealth and some top Government ministers were told that a Royal wedding was on the cards, possibly during mid-summer.

Christmas separated the couple again. Diana caught a bad dose of 'flu and went to her father's at Althorp for the festivities. Charles spent Christmas Day with the rest of the Royal Family at Windsor and then joined them for their ritual pilgrimage to Sandringham. It had become a tradition for the Royal Family to spend the New Year and most of January at Sandringham, shooting pheasants and riding on the 20,000 acre estate. It had also been a tradition that they were to be left completely alone during this time. In past years the Queen's Press Secretary had written to Fleet Street editors asking them to respect the Royal privacy over their Sandringham holiday. This New Year the polite request was completely ignored. Hordes of reporters and photographers were dispatched to Norfolk. The year of 1981 began with the Royal Family under virtual siege. As world interest intensified, the crowd of warmly-wrapped men camping out in their cars in front of the main gates swelled to fifty at times; the Royal Family began to lose their tempers. Angry words were exchanged and there was even talk that a Royal shotgun had been discharged dangerously close to some of the over-eager scribes and spent pellets rattled down on the roofs of their cars.

Lady Diana, who had been invited to join the rest of the Royal Family at this time, had to stay away. Through her press secretary the Queen showed her displeasure: "The Queen is angry at what she considers is an intrusion of her privacy." Prince Charles joined in, wishing a group of clicking photographers a "very happy new year", and adding, "I hope your editors have a particularly nasty one." Even young Prince Edward, aged sixteen, showed a bit of schoolboyish bad humour shouting: "Watch out, you might get shot" to photographers getting a little too close for comfort. At this a number of Fleet Street editors got cold feet and pulled out their men. Only a couple of the more sensational tabloids kept their men on after the Royal outburst. Before dawn on the bitterly cold morning of 7 January, Charles sneaked away from Sandringham unnoticed by the remaining small press posse who by now had found warm hotel rooms in nearby King's Lynn. He drove across country to Gloucestershire to meet with Lady Diana at their usual spot, Highgrove. They spent that evening together before a log fire in one of the almost bare reception rooms. Diana had driven down to Highgrove in her newest acquisition, a pillar box red brand new Mini Metro. It was rumoured, but later denied, that the car, one of the first to be seen on British roads, had been bought for Diana by Prince Charles. But it is significant that the car was purchased from a garage which services and maintains Royal vehicles.

It was another early start the next morning, and at 5.30 a.m. the couple drove in convoy fifty miles east along the M4 motorway from Tetbury, he in his Ford estate with his detective and she following behind in her new mini.

Charles had been in the habit of riding his magnificent racehorse Allibar across the Berkshire downs at dawn, training for the next race. He was booked to ride at Chepstow in February. Diana, in thick sweater and green waterproof coat stood for more than an hour on the edge of the downs watching the Prince put Allibar through his paces. Then a detective drove Diana to breakfast and after putting his horse back in its stable box and slipping the animal the usual couple of sugar lumps, the Prince borrowed an old bicycle and peddled off to join her.

The couple had been invited to breakfast with the Prince's racehorse trainer Nick Gaselee. It had become a regular feature of the Prince's cold dawn rides, boiled eggs, toast and tea to warm him up at 7 a.m. But the fun of breakfast in the Gaselee's kitchen was rudely shattered by the sound of car doors slamming in the quiet lane outside. Diana and Charles had not covered their tracks well enough. Two photographers had driven down from London at dawn, just on the offchance when they spotted that Diana's distinctive red car was not parked outside her flat. Now, cameras at the ready, they stood guard outside the white painted 200-year-old cottage knowing that Charles and Diana were inside. Since September, Charles had been determined that no one would get a photograph of him with Lady Diana: it had almost become something of an obsession. He believed that the press had contributed to the ending of his affairs in the past by hounding girls mercilessly and he was not going to let that happen to Lady Diana.

"My, you are up early this morning gentlemen," he said sarcastically to the two cameramen as they photographed him emerging from the cottage door. He had stayed in the warm for fifteen minutes after Lady Diana left to give her the chance to get clean away. Diana had

38

been photographed coming out of the same door but not in the same frame. In fact through clever planning they were not photographed together at any time during their courtship. The first pictures were the official ones on the terrace at the back of Buckingham Palace the day of the announcement. But to secure their privacy Diana was to undergo some indignity during the next six weeks. (On one occasion she was even forced to lie in the back of a landrover covered by a blanket to escape the cameras. "Not exactly the way to treat a lady," observed the *Daily Mirror*.) Diana drove back to London and the seclusion of her flat. For the next few days she tried to continue life as normal, kindergarten during the day and suppers with her flatmates before an evening of television.

Meanwhile the press were back in force at Sandringham. The Queen had asked Charles to formulate some plan to lure them away. Charles suggested to Diana, in one of his late night phone calls, that she should go home to Althorp for the week-end, and drop a hint to the press of her destination. On Friday night Diana drove North up the M1 motorway to Northampton and Althorp. One of the flatmates, who so dutifully guarded their friend, carefully dropped the name Althorp to the first of the many journalists who were always on the phone. That week-end visitors to the house who had paid their £1 were not disappointed. Lady Diana was spotted walking alone through woodland on the estate, warmly wrapped against the cold in a green coat and boots and incongruously, an old man's trilby hat. On Sunday evening Diana drove back home to her flat after her week-end away from it all. One more day of peace and quiet was all she would get before being flung once more headlong into subterfuge and controversy.

Most of the Royal Family, including Charles, were still

at Sandringham for their New Year holidays. Diana still had that outstanding invitation from the Queen to join them all for a few days and the lady was determined to go to Norfolk. Under cover of darkness she drove east out of London, but cleverly not in her own car. She left her flat in the red mini metro but switched, in the grounds of Kensington Palace, where her sister Jane lives, to a borrowed silver Volkswagen Golf. Diana knew Sandringham like the back of her hand after a childhood spent in a rented home on the Royal Estate. By dinner time she was safely inside dining with the Royal Family. Later that morning, boldly in broad daylight, Lady Diana drove straight past the unsuspecting watchers and headed back into London but not without some help from the rest of the Royal Family. A neat little plot was hatched to lure the press party away and let Diana escape. Some of the Royal males, Prince Philip and Princess Anne's husband Captain Mark Phillips, went off for a pheasant shoot, distracting about a third of the photographers. Meanwhile Prince Charles drove quickly and noisily past the thirty or so reporters and cameramen still clustered round the main gate. They gave chase only to find that he had gone to the dog kennels by a side gate to feed his labrador Harvey. The Prince smiled knowingly as the photographers had to content themselves with just the Prince. Charles knew that as they wasted film on him Lady Diana was driving out of a side gate back to London and her flat. She was home by one p.m. – the press had been beaten again.

The Royal Family met for lunch in a privately booked room at a local public house, aptly named the King's Head. The sound of their laughter could be heard in the saloon bar where the journalists were drowning their sorrows. Even Princess Anne had earlier wound down her car window to say with a sly smile "She's gone you know." When Charles finished his pub lunch there was a gloating tone in his voice when he said: "There is no one here. I wish you would all go away." The crestfallen bunch of pressmen took him at his word and headed off along the road taken earlier by Lady Diana. There was nothing left for them at Sandringham now. The next confrontation would not be much more successful for them either.

Before Christmas Charles had discussed with Diana the possibility of taking a skiing holiday together. It was a slightly embarrassing invitation for him to make because three years earlier, while Diana was still a schoolgirl, the Prince had taken her elder red-headed sister, Lady Sarah, to the snows of the Swiss Alps for a ten-day chalet holiday in the village of Klosters. But Diana, who was a competent skier after a few earlier ski resort holidays with schoolfriends and her family, accepted the Prince's invitation without hesitation. It sounded like a lot of fun. In the event Charles flew off to Zurich without her on 23 January. As world interest had hotted up the couple had realised how impractical a normal holiday would become. Anyway, it would have ruined the Prince's determination not to be photographed with her.

For the next ten days the Prince, in a navy ski suit and woolly hat, zoomed up and down the piste staying in the chalet, which is owned by his old friends Charles Palmer Tomkinson and his wife Patti. He took part in a long distance cross-country race and won a cow bell as a prize – and he phoned Diana every night. He had made up his mind. He would propose marriage to Lady Diana Frances Spencer formally as soon as he returned to Britain.

Chapter Four

BORN TO BE QUEEN

The future Queen of England was born in the middle of the hottest afternoon for years. She was a perfectly formed, healthy bouncing seven pound baby and her parents, Frances and Johnny, were both delighted of course with the latest addition to their family. They already had two daughters and they had lost a baby son tragically. They had hoped and prayed for another son, a future heir for the considerable family fortune, and on this afternoon, the first day of July 1961 they had not thought of one single girl's name in expectation of a boy. But the new baby took her first public engagement calmly and without tears as she was christened Diana Frances Spencer in a Norfolk parish church. As if in anticipation of her destiny in just nineteen years, she was born on land and property owned by the British Royal Family. The large country home, Park House, was just a stone's throw from Sandringham.

With an illustrious lineage which stretched all the way back to the rule of Charles II, Diana was born, like her older sisters Jane and Sarah, with an automatic title. Diana's family were distantly related to the Royal Family, and her father, Edward, the eighth Earl Spencer, known as "Johnny" to his family, was very close friends with the Queen and Prince Philip. He was also an equerry to the

Queen. Living on the Sandringham estate, Diana virtually grew up with the Royal children. There was just a low dry stone wall to separate their homes and the three princes and their princess sister would regularly climb over to share the small open air swimming pool at Park House. Her regular playmate was Prince Andrew, an angelic looking boy two years older than herself. Looking back now, Diana cannot remember meeting the much older, and to her as a little girl somewhat mysterious, Prince Charles. As Diana grew up at Park House, Charles was away at preparatory or boarding school. He must have first seen her when she was still in nappies and he was a thirteen or fourteen-year-old schoolboy heading rapidly for manhood.

She was there, right under his nose, most of his life, but he just didn't notice her. Neither Charles nor Diana can really remember meeting before November 1977, the year of the Queen's Silver Jubilee. The Spencers, their family split by the trauma of divorce, had by then moved to their ancestral home, Althorp in Northamptonshire. It was Diana's older sister Sarah, who introduced the two as they stood in a muddy ploughed field. Charles had come to Althorp for a day's hunting and he recalled later thinking at the time "what a very jolly, amusing and attractive sixteen-year-old". Although he would meet her on a number of other occasions it would be three years before the courtship really began.

Diana is remembered as a toddler who grew up to be a trouble free, happy child. Her first governess, Gertrude Allen, now in her seventies, patiently and dutifully read and listened to the infant Diana in the nursery at Park House. "A very conscientious child, she would always try," recalled Miss Allen. That is how everyone remembers the little girl with the bright blue eyes and the sort of

English peaches-and-cream complexion that ladies of other nations would murder for. Diana was always thoughtful, the sort of little girl who was always the first to put a log on the fire, a practical girl who would go round Park House in winter closing the shutters. Diana remembers her childhood at Park House as "a good time of my life". She was too young to remember the unhappiness and heartbreak which split the Spencer family in 1967.

Edward John Spencer's marriage to the fourth Baron Fermoy's daughter, Frances in 1954, was the wedding of the year. Diana's mother was only eighteen-years-old when she walked up the aisle of Westminster Abbey. Almost every member of the Royal Family, led by the Queen and Prince Philip, were there that day. An unlucky thirteen years later, after bearing four children (Sarah then aged twelve, Jane, ten, Diana six, and the latest addition Charles only three-years-old), Frances decided at the age of thirty-one that she had to find a new life. One day, a servant remembers, Diana's mother "just was not there any more". Her decision to leave her husband and family created a national scandal at the time, and made the two oldest girls, Sarah and Jane desperately unhappy. Diana would only be told as a teenager of the divorce in 1969, when the arguments and rows over the custody of the children split both Frances' family, the Fermoys, and the Spencers, right down the middle. Even today, Frances, now Mrs. Shand-Kydd will not discuss the bitterness of 1969. That same year she married Peter Shand-Kydd, whose wealthy family owned a giant wallpaper business.

The divorce meant that the four Spencer children saw their mother only rarely, but they all adored their father who had won the court case for their custody. But as Diana grew, so did the emotional links between mother and daughter. Frances' influence was to grow stronger in Diana's adolescent years. Her father lived a solitary life until 1976 when he married Raine, Countess of Dartmouth, the daughter of best-selling romantic novelist Barbara Cartland. The trauma of the divorce came and went relatively unnoticed by the little girl as she moved on to school, first at Riddlesworth Hall, a private preparatory school in Diss, Norfolk, not far from Park House, and then to West Heath, a boarding school in Kent. During her holidays she played with the young Royal set from next door and became used to meeting the Queen and Prince Philip in a way that meant she was never in awe of them. To Diana it was rather like meeting one's father's bosses, and her relaxed attitude in their company would pave the way for the romance of 1980.

At West Heath, and later at a Swiss finishing school, Diana received a typical British middle-class education, but not an intellectual one. Her school friends remember her as a fun-loving, easy-going and considerate girl, the kind of person who never forgot to send birthday cards on the right day. Her interests were looking after young children, swimming, classical music, ballet and later ski-ing. A typical school report for the West Heath academy where Diana studied between 1973 and 1977 would have revealed that she had average marks in English, but showed a keen interest in history – understandably with her family background. She had a natural talent for art lessons and was an excellent pupil in the dance classes. Just a few months before her courtship started in earnest Diana tried to teach Charles how to tap dance on a con-crete terrace at Sandringham; her lesson ended with them both roaring with laughter. At school she slept with a picture of Prince Charles above her bed. The placing of the photograph was a very strange coincidence, especially in view of the way things turned out. The photograph, of the Prince's investiture as Prince of Wales in 1969, was presented to the school by former newspaper chief Cecil King, whose grand-daughter was a pupil. The picture became a favourite with Diana and the girls who shared her plain white-painted dormitory. The photograph is still hanging in the room to this day.

Headmistress, Miss Ruth Rudge, remembers that Diana was a delight to have at the school. She was so popular that on her leaving day she was presented with a cup for special services to the school. "She was always helpful and willing," recalled Miss Rudge. "The dining room staff liked her a lot because she used to help them with laying tables and clearing up." Life at school was quite spartan. At 7.30 a.m. sharp the rising bell would ring. Lessons continued until 7.00 p.m. with an extra session on Saturday morning. Lady Diana remembers West Heath as "a thoroughly enjoyable time". While she was still at school her father and her sisters had left the ten-bedroomed Park House for much bigger surroundings at Althorp. In 1975 Edward Spencer inherited the family seat from his father, Jack, becoming the eighth Earl. The sixteenth century stately house at Althorp is one of Britain's best kept houses and it contains the cream of the contents of five homes once owned by the Spencer family. The house is filled with pictures by Rubens, Poussin, Van Dyke, Gainsborough, Reynolds, Lely and many others. There is also some fine furniture and extensive collections of porcelain and silver. For Diana, her two older sisters and her younger brother Charles, it was like moving into a museum. Diana was sharing her holidays between Althorp and her mother's new home on the Scottish Island of Seil where her new stepfather ran a beef farm. Her relationship with her mother was growing closer and closer. There had been a remarkable similarity between them always. They look very much alike physically, with the same height, 5 ft. 10 ins., and build. Both were to become engaged in their teens to glamorous men.

It was during this time of getting used to living in Althorp and flitting between Northamptonshire, her school in Kent and her mother in Scotland, that her future stepmother entered her life. Raine Dartmouth's arrival at Althorp sparked off quite a stir among the Spencer children. Raine was like a heroine from one of her mother's, Barbara Cartland's, novels. At the age of eighteen she had been married to a handsome guards officer, Gerald Legge, who later became the Earl of Dartmouth. Lady Diana's father was at Eton with him. A slim, health fanatic with a porcelain complexion, Raine had boundless energy. At the age of twenty-three she became Westminster's youngest councillor and was famous all over Britain for her welfare work. In 1976, the year after Edward became Earl Spencer, Raine parted from the man she used to describe as "so steady and strong" and moved into Althorp to be with her husband's old school friend. The Earl of Dartmouth cited Lady Diana's father in the divorce action which followed, but the judge granted a decree because of Raine's "adultery with a man against whom the charge has not been proved". Two months after the divorce Raine became Countess Spencer. All four Spencer children, including Diana, stayed away from the ceremony which was a very small affair with only two witnesses. Even Barbara Cartland wasn't invited. Her daughter just rang her after the ceremony to say "Hello, we're married".

Diana saw little of her stepmother, but Lady Sarah

made her feelings very clear by telling a gossip writer, "Lady Dartmouth is an all-too frequent visitor." Raine told Barbara Cartland, "They won't accept me. Whatever I do is wrong. I just want us to be one close family." To help pay off some of the immense death duties incurred by the death of the seventh Earl Spencer, Raine went about revamping the house. She opened the house to the public offering guided tours and had a souvenir shop built in the stable block. She even employed staff to open an afternoon tea bar to encourage the day trippers. All this did not go down too well with the Spencer children.

But then near tragedy brought the family together and the children, even Sarah, began to see another side to Raine. She became literally a lifesaver to their father and all the children had cause to thank her. Just a few days after holding a party celebrating his return to a position of credit at the bank, the Earl collapsed in the stable yard with a massive brain haemorrhage. He was rushed to Northampton Hospital where doctors told Raine he was unlikely to survive the night. She refused to believe this and immediately chartered a private ambulance to dash seventy miles to a special brain clinic in London. She then began a long fight to save his life, swapping doctors and hospitals in her determination. "I wanted to use my life and my energy for his life," she said later. Sitting beside his bed for hours on end she cajoled and nagged her husband back to life. One day she played him a tape of one of his favourite operas, 'Madame Butterfly', and quite suddenly he just opened his eyes and came out of a long coma. He said later that through his coma he had heard everything that Raine had said to him. Now there is little to show for his near brush with death, just a slight blurring of his voice, an occasional speech hesitation. The

An official engagement picture.

Golden wedding anniversary of Lady Diana's grandparents,
with Lady Diana as a little girl *(front centre)*.

Lady Diana as a bridesmaid at her eldest sister's wedding.

Left: Prince Charles in a play at Cambridge University during his student days.

Below: Prince Charles at Cambridge, 1968.

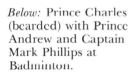

Right: Prince Charles on a commando course at Lympstone, Devon, November 1974.

Below: Prince Charles (bearded) with Prince Andrew and Captain Mark Phillips at Badminton.

Above: Members of Lady Diana's family at a wedding.

Below: Lady Diana's father, Earl Spencer, in the grounds of Althorp, the family home.

Mrs Frances Shand-Kydd at home (mother of Lady Diana).

Above: The outside of Highgrove House, Prince Charles' home in the Cotswolds, 1980.

Below: The yellow bedroom at Highgrove House.

Spencer girls, who are all devoted to their father, were delighted by what Raine had achieved.

By 1978 Lady Diana, sixteen-years-old and fresh out of West Heath school, was at the exclusive Institut Alpin Videmanette in Rougemont, Switzerland, a very expensive finishing school for young ladies. While she was at the school, improving her skiing and learning social poise and grace, her sister was in the same Swiss Alps at Klosters holidaying with Prince Charles. The holiday was the talk of the press and the school, but Diana never spoke of it. Diana was improving her already good grasp of the French language and her teacher, Madame Barbara Fuls, recalled that "while Diana was a pretty girl she was not the beauty she's blossomed into now. She knew she wanted to work with children, to get married and have a family of her own, and she once told me that she would only marry for love not for money or position." During her brief stay at the Institut, Diana took domestic science and learned the art of dressmaking and cooking, mainly French or Swiss, certainly not the roast beef of old England. But she did not last the full course in Switzerland. Suffering from a severe bout of homesickness, she returned to Britain after only two months. Her father decided she should have her freedom and bought her a London flat, the home she was to have for two years until her engagement to Prince Charles. Diana moved in, gathering round her the three girls who were to become her closest friends and confidantes.

Just like her sisters, Diana had decided, despite her social status, she did not want to be a debutante. Becoming a "deb" is the unique English ritual involving the introduction of a young woman into London society. It involves an expensive round of parties, dances and afternoon teas, a tradition with origins deeply rooted in the upper classes. Diana wanted none of this; instead of being heralded into society she took the job she had always wanted, looking after children in a kindergarten. Her character and her way of life were now well formed and she had grown into a beautiful young woman. She was no longer the slightly rounded, giggly schoolgirl Prince Charles remembered.

Diana had developed into a fresh, deceptively unsophisticated girl, warm, reliable, quick witted, open hearted and very attractive. But strangely enough during this time of freedom in one of the liveliest capitals in the world, Diana never had a steady boyfriend. She went out on occasional dates but they were purely platonic friendships. As her uncle, Lord Fermoy, put it very bluntly, "She has had no lovers."

The only word Diana ever objected to being called was "sweet", she didn't mind being variously described as shy, innocent, modest or even quiet, but she did object to that word "sweet" – "I'm a normal person," she would tell reporters, "and I love life."

According to one of her friends, Old Etonian Simon Berry, aged twenty-three, whose parents run a London wine business, Lady Diana broke the hearts of dozens of young men during the two years she lived in Coleherne Court. "Chaps would meet Diana and fall instantly in love," he said. "Many tried to win her, sending flowers and begging for a date, but she always politely declined." Diana was never one for discos or parties. Occasional meals at her favourite London restaurant, the Poule au Pot in Ebury Street, Victoria, where she would dine with a group, or private dinner parties at the homes of friends were the usual way, she spent a night out. She seemed to love cosy evenings at home with her friends. She chose her friends very carefully, almost as if she were planning for a future in which her past would be closely examined. All her chosen companions were well bred, well educated and totally trustworthy.

What Diana is instantly remembered for is her tremendous sense of humour. Like Prince Charles, Diana seems to revel in a good practical joke and pranks to be played on her friends like doing impressions of Miss Piggy in the Muppets television series over the telephone. During their brief courtship Charles and Diana would roar with laughter together over a brilliant little send up of them in the British satirical magazine *Private Eye*. The *Eye* wrote about their romance in a mushy manner under the byline 'Silvie Krin'. In the regular fortnightly features Diana was always looking at Charles with limpid eyes while he only had evil thoughts on how to deprive her of her virginity. Charles had kept all the issues and together they would read them again and again, delighted by the wicked humour. Like Charles, Diana had acquired a liking for the arts and for music; she plays the piano a little, he the cello. She had learned to love driving, passing her test at the age of eighteen. Again, like the man she was to marry, she rarely drinks, except for a glass of wine, and she has never smoked. It was her driving which gave a clue to a hitherto unseen side to Lady Diana Spencer. As soon as she passed her test she gained a reputation as a demon driver. She was involved in three minor accidents in the first year she coped with the pressures of the fierce London traffic. Her first car, a light blue Volkswagen Polo, always seemed to be off the road for repairs to a new dent or scrape and photographers chasing her at the start of the Royal courtship discovered that she enjoyed a good snarl at other drivers who were not quick enough for her as she whipped crisply round central London.

Lady Diana Frances Spencer had grown up to be a woman with a mind of her own as well as a natural beauty. Even before her engagement the much photographed Spencer glossy fringe from which she peeped out shyly at the world was being copied in hair stylists' salons all over Britain. Thousands of young girls have adopted her honey blonde hairstyle. Although she is a very wealthy young lady, Diana's teenage clothes style was never extravagant. It was not the usual Gucci, Pucci and Fiorucci. She was never caught in anything more outré than a pair of corduroy culottes, a borrowed sweatshirt or a man's corduroy smoking jacket. But she is doomed to a life of flat shoes. High heels are out for a girl who is as tall as her fiancé: it wouldn't be protocol to tower over the future King.

Chapter Five

BORN TO BE KING

The bridegroom's formal title is His Royal Highness the Prince Charles Philip Arthur George, Prince of Wales and Earl of Chester, Duke of Cornwall and Rothesay, Earl of Carrick and Baron of Renfrew, Lord of the Isles and Great Steward of Scotland, Knight of The Garter. The Prince of Wales and Earl of Chester are joint titles most closely associated with a male heir apparent of a reigning monarch. They go back to Edward II who had them conferred on him in February 1301. On the death of a Prince of Wales and Earl of Chester in the lifetime of a sovereign the titles do not pass on to the current holder's son. They must be recreated with each reign. Cornwall and the five Scottish titles came, by tradition, to Charles as eldest son of the sovereign, from the moment the Queen ascended to the throne. Edward III created his son Duke of Cornwall in March 1337 making it clear that the title should descend to the eldest son of the kings and queens of England forever. The Scottish titles go back to the seventeenth century. They were brought to England when James the Sixth of Scotland became James the First of England after the death of the first Queen Elizabeth. Charles is now the holder of them as heir to the old kingdom of Scotland.

He was born at Buckingham Palace on the evening of

14 November, 1948, the first male in direct succession for more than eighty years. His ancestors include such unlikely figures as the first president of the United States, George Washington, and the Prophet of Islam, Mohammed. As Prince of Wales he is in the ancestral line of a pageant of royalty that includes Edward, the classical armour-clad Black Prince of the fourteenth century – who used to feature in so many Hollywood epics starring either Robert Taylor or Tony Curtis – the marriage-prone Henry VIII, and the man who gave his name to both a style of living and an era, Queen Victoria's son, Edward VII. Discovery of his fate came to Charles when he was about eight-years-old, "in the most ghastly, inexorable sense". He remembers: "I didn't suddenly wake up in my pram one day and say 'Yippee'. I think it just dawns on you slowly, that people are interested in you and you slowly get the idea that you have a certain duty and responsibility. I think it's better that way, rather than someone suddenly telling you." He knows he will one day represent an institution constantly under attack, and that he will be king of a country that has known better days. He has a great faith in Britain, however, and a strong belief in what the country still stands for.

In childhood Charles was somewhat shy and introverted, in contrast to Anne, who was ebullient and outward going. As a toddler he would snuggle up beside his mother on a settee and look quietly at a picture book, or listen to her as she read him a story. The most popular ones were the *Tales of Beatrix Potter* and the adventures of *Baba the Elephant* and *Tin-Tin*. He had enough boyish spirit in him, however, for the Queen, just like any other mother, to have to cope with the pranks and mischief of her son. He raced round the corridors of Buckingham Palace with his friends, played risky games of hide-and-seek on the roof of Windsor Castle, or slipped pieces of ice down the collar of a footman. When he deserved it he would get a good spanking, particularly if he was caught being rude to the servants. The Queen took a very stern view of this. Her Majesty also taught him the value of money, restricting his pocket money to the equivalent of twelve pence a week until he was ten-years-old, when he was given a rise which made it twenty-five pence. As part of the training for a ceremonial life, Charles and Anne were taught to stand motionless for long periods, to accustom them to the duties ahead.

Hundreds of requests came for the young Prince to make public appearances but the Queen resisted them all, no matter how worthy the cause. She remembered how, as a young princess in the war years, she was suddenly thrust into the public arena and she insisted that her son should first of all have a normal childhood, as far as this could be arranged. So the Queen protected Charles and brought him up carefully to the stage when he was gradually made aware of his state duties. Her Majesty was also determined that her son would not become a palace wastrel, a mere understudy, deprived of any responsibility and forever waiting in the wings. She had seen too much of this in the history of her family. Charles was to be made aware of his future role at the right time, then be prepared for it.

The Queen took special care over the education of the Prince. Sending Charles away to school, rather than having the traditional private tuition for him, was to set a royal precedent. She decided that, unlike his predecessors, he should go out and meet his future subjects. Her Majesty had been educated behind the railings of Buckingham Palace by a succession of governesses and tutors. Charles was given the chance to go beyond the royal stockade, and live among ordinary people. She helped her son through all the usual growing pains of youth and his moments of bewilderment at life. Her encouragement was always there whenever he thought the going was too tough. When he first went away to school she wrote to him almost daily, feeding him family gossip to keep up his spirits. At university Charles occasionally found the task a struggle and felt lonely. The Queen would visit him privately in his rooms at Trinity College, where they would talk over his problems while he fried a simple meal for the two of them.

The Queen attended to her son's upbringing with a typical mother's gentleness but Prince Philip provided a grittier influence. The late George V once said: "My father was frightened of his father . . . I was frightened of my father . . . and I'm going to see to it that my children are frightened of me." Royal paternal attitudes have changed considerably since the beginning of this century, when that Royal view was expressed. Charles and Philip have a very close relationship, based not on fear, but on love and respect for each other's achievements. Their personalities differ considerably. Prince Philip has always been the more abrasive while Charles has more gentleness of spirit. One of the Duke's friends once said: "Charles is not a bit like him." At first Charles seemed to try hard to emulate his father. He was tempted to adopt Philip's occasional high-handed style. But as he grew out of his teens the Prince developed a likeable personality of his own, while his father began to mellow. They tend to have the same mannerisms: the brisk walk, the habit of clenching their hands behind their backs, and tossing their heads when laughing; Charles, too, walks around with his left hand thrust casually into his jacket pocket. He has inherited his father's sense of humour; both like zany, outrageous slapstick rather than sharpness of wit.

Otherwise their tastes are usually quite different. Charles adores music for instance, whereas Prince Philip often finds it a trial to have to sit through a concert. The young Prince can enjoy solitary pastimes, while the Duke is much more gregarious. Some people close to the family think Princess Anne, Prince Andrew and Prince Edward take more after their father than the eldest son. When Charles was a child, Prince Philip was determined that his son would not have a pampered life. When Charles was a schoolboy, Philip once noticed a servant hurrying to close a door that his son had failed to shut. He shouted: "Leave it alone. He's got hands. He can go back and do it himself." Like the Queen, Prince Philip wanted him to rub up against other children, and to see how others lived. He said: "We want him to go to school with other boys of his generation and to learn to live with other children. To absorb from his childhood the discipline imposed by education with others." He also wanted Charles to pick up a few bruises and get used to the hard knocks of tough physical activities. Dancing lessons were stopped, music lessons cut down and, instead, Charles was sent off to the playing field in Chelsea to get into the rough and tumble of soccer with other youngsters. He also went to a private gymnasium twice a week for gymnastic work-outs.

Prince Philip took him out in bitter wintry weather to teach him to shoot in the mud and puddles of marshes and over the heather around Balmoral, where Charles shot his first grouse when he was ten-years-old. He taught him how to fish as well. When Philip was at home he would spend an hour after tea teaching his son to swim in the pool at Buckingham Palace. Charles took to the water without a hint of nervousness and could swim a length before he was five-years-old. Father and son would have a boisterous game of football in the palace grounds, with the corgis barking round their heels. Now and again the Queen and toddler Anne might join in the fun. Nearly all his physical skills were taught to Charles by his father. In this way they grew closer to each other, and Philip was delighted to see his son developing into a self-confident youngster. But Charles has never had the Duke's ambition to excel at organised games. He still shows little enthusiasm for team games, such as rugby, soccer and cricket. Individual achievement, where he is testing himself rather than others, has been his forte, hence the generally solitary pursuits he tends to go in for . . . diving, surfing, flying. His only concession to 'team spirit' is polo.

Philip introduced his son to sailing, but Charles did not develop the same passion for it as his father, and the two rarely go sailing together these days because they do not seem to see eye-to-eye when they are in a boat. Charles explains frankly: "I remember one disastrous day when we were racing and my father was shouting instructions. We wound the winch harder and the sail split in half with a sickening crack. Father was not pleased. Not long after that I was banned from the boat after an incident cruising off Scotland. There was no wind and I was amusing myself taking pot-shots at beer cans floating around the boat. The only gust of the day blew the jib in front of my rifle just as I fired. I wasn't invited back on board." The Duke in consultation with the Queen and her advisers, also influenced the choice of schools for their offspring. He had his way first over the preparatory school Charles went to before moving on to public school. Philip attended Cheam School, which is set in sixty-five acres of grounds on the Berkshire border. It has a history of teaching the aristocracy and the sons of the rich going back as far as the early seventeenth century. Charles, too was sent there.

The really decisive part played by the royal father in helping to bring out the manly qualities in Charles was when the time came to select a senior school for him. Eton, the traditional establishment for top young English gentlemen, was, at first, favoured by the Queen. Charles' name had been put down for a place when he was born. Philip had other ideas. He wanted – and got – his own *alma mater*: tough, authoritarian Gordonstoun set in a bleak stretch of Northern Scotland in Morayshire and based on the principles of the German educationalist Dr. Kurt Hahn. Gordonstoun had been good enough for the Duke. He thought its harsh, cold-shower regime had done him a world of good, so why should it not do the same for his eldest son? When the young Prince went there he was still fairly shy and withdrawn. Charles remembers now that all the tales he had heard about it made the school seem "pretty gruesome". It was a very nervous young man who was flown by his father up to Morayshire to start his few bracing years there. Philip reminded him "not to let the side down".

The place was mainly a collection of crude huts. Charles' dormitory had unpainted wooden walls, bare floors and uncomfortable iron beds. There was the obligatory cold shower to be taken every morning, no matter what the weather. As the school is situated in one of the more exposed and rugged parts of Scotland, the temperature was usually at shivering level. Even the school motto – *'Plus est en vous'* (There is more in you) – typified a harsh system aimed at stretching to the full both physical and intellectual capabilities. To bring him down to earth and away from any fancy ideas he might have of being a special sort of fellow from the land of palaces, his housemaster gave Charles a particularly humiliating daily task in his first term – emptying the dustbins. Charles may have been reluctant to be submitted to the rigours of Gordonstoun, but he never quarrelled with his father's decision. He disliked the school at first, became terribly homesick and did not fit easily into the regime. After four years Charles ended up loving the place, just as his father had done. He became head boy and, shrugging his shoulders, pointed out that it was not really as tough as he had expected it to be. He excelled in geography and modern languages, captained the school's cricket and hockey teams and represented Gordonstoun in inter-school athletics meetings. He also took the title role in a production of 'Macbeth'. Charles has a fascination for history which he carried with him from Gordonstoun to Trinity College, Cambridge, where he studied archaeology and anthropology during his first year. He had an average Class II Division I pass in his tripos on these subjects before switching to modern history for his last two years at university, at the end of which he took a Bachelor of Arts Honours degree. "When you meet as many people as I do, you become curious about what makes men tick and what makes men tick differently." His exam papers are preserved for posterity in the royal library at Windsor. His tutor on social anthropology commented in a supervision report: "He writes useful and thoughtful essays, although sometimes they are a little rushed. He is interested in discussion – likes to draw parallels between the peoples we study and ourselves."

At Cambridge he also developed a love for the stage and knock-about farce. He appeared in undergraduate revues, and earned himself the nickname 'Clown

Prince'. He has links with Australia that go back to his schooldays, when he spent a year at Timbertops – the abrasive, open-air school in the mountains north of Melbourne. He has returned to Australia regularly ever since. With his love of risking his neck now and again, he goes down well with a people who like a man to prove his courage. He regards the year he spent at school in Australia as "the most wonderful period" in his life. The Australians responded to his affection for their country and themselves with such endearing terms as: "Good on yer, Pommy bastard." Part of his transition from nervous teenager to confident man took place there; away from the protecting arms of his family he learned to stand alone.

The Prince's liking for swimming fits in perfectly with Australia's beach-side way of life. When he paid an official visit in 1974 he spent as much time as possible in the sometimes treacherous, rolling seas. At Coolangatta he watched local beach rescue squads in operation in the risky surf. He persuaded the beach guards and anxious local officials to allow him to ride in a powerful new rescue craft. Once in the boat he took over the controls himself, and flew across the waves.

During that tour of Australia and New Zealand he rolled up his sleeves and joined the sheep shearers. These men, who earn their living clipping wool to clothe people throughout the world, are among the toughest and roughest workers anywhere. Charles took to them immediately, and they to him, when he called at a sheep station near Wellington, New Zealand. Their way of life interested him. He asked them about their homes, their families, and what they wanted in the future. Then the 'gaffer' of the shearers asked Charles to lend a hand. A dozen or so bewildered beasts were brought up and

H.R.H. swung into action with a pole, pushing the sheep through a murky, foul-smelling dip. It was a bit of a struggle and he doubted whether he could ever have earned a week's wages on the job. But he learned a little more about one tiny part of his future dominion.

The Queen made Charles a Knight of The Garter, one of the oldest orders of chivalry in the world, when he was ten-years-old, but he was not invested and installed in the Royal Chapel at Windsor until 1968, when he reached the age of twenty. One of his first formal steps towards the eventual responsibility of the throne was in the autumn of 1972 when, at the age of twenty-three, he was appointed a Councillor of State – together with the Queen Mother – to handle the official affairs of the realm while the Queen visited Australia. This function is vital to the running of Britain and the Commonwealth because, constitutionally, the works of governments at home and abroad have to be officially approved by the sovereign or her properly appointed representatives.

Charles' interest in the social conditions of modern life, his awareness of community problems, and concern for the well-being of the nation have been demonstrated in his work for Wales. When the Queen and Prince Philip decided the time had come for Charles to take up the title of Prince of Wales, they were determined that, unlike the late Duke of Windsor when he bore the same name, their son was to develop more than just a nodding acquaintance with the place. He was to learn the Welsh language and culture and the history of the principality. His involvement in all things Welsh now includes being Colonel-in-Chief of the Welsh Guards, the youngest regiment of the Brigade of Guards. It is in their uniform that he rides with his mother every June to take part in that most spectacular ceremony of Trooping the Colour, on Horse Guards Parade in London. He first donned the white-plumed bearskin and scarlet jacket for this celebration of the sovereign's official birthday while he was in the Royal Navy in 1975. Since then, and for the future, it has become one of the most important yearly engagements in his diary.

This mounting involvement in public events has taken the heir closer to millions on a global scale. He feels nothing is too much trouble if it helps him to establish a link with those he will rule.

Chapter Six

CHARLIE'S GIRLS

Lady Diana, like the rest of the world, has known about Prince Charles' reputation as a ladies' man. After all, even her own elder sister, Lady Sarah, was one of the Charlie Set – or Charlie's Angels as some people called them – for two years. And it was through Lady Sarah that Charles first met Diana. Charles' string of polo ponies could never match his string of girl friends. They ranged from his first love, while he was at Cambridge University as an eighteen-year-old, the stunning dark-haired Chilean Lucia Santa Cruz, to the sexy blonde British actress Susan George . . . one of the latest Charlie Girls before the engagement. Over the years he had girl friends in many parts of the world, most of whom remained friends and kept happy memories of their relationships.

Throughout his many years of discreet meetings in the country, on desert islands or quietly in his apartments at Buckingham Palace Charles had the pick of the best. But while Prince Charles was, at last, showing off to the world his future bride in the garden at the back of Buckingham Palace on their engagement day the Band of the Coldstream Guards marched to the front playing 'Now your philandering days are over!' This song from the *Marriage of Figaro* seemed very appropriate, because one thing is for certain – Charles is going to have to change his life style after the Royal Wedding. Having a string of girlfriends might not be unusual for any other eligible bachelor, but with Charles every one of them was brought into the national queen-spotting game. He admits that occasionally he looks at one of his regular companions and asks himself: "I wonder if I could ever marry her?" The Prince had always said that he would get married when he was "around thirty" and he had very down-to-earth views about committing himself. His marriage had to be for keeps, without any question of subsequent divorce. He regarded it as a frightening decision because of the special need, in his case, to find the right partner to live with in harmony. "I hope I will be as lucky as my own parents who have been so happy," he once said, and another time told an interviewer: "Marriage is a much more important business than falling in love. I think it is essentially a question of mutual love and respect for each other. Creating a secure family unit in which to bring up children and give them a happy, secure upbringing, that is what marriage is all about – creating a home."

When he cast his eyes around the world's palaces he had precious little to choose from. There was a dearth of princesses waiting in their ivory towers for Charles to come whirling in by helicopter and whizz them away. There were hardly any in the same age group or with the same interests as the British prince. A few tentative steps were taken by Prince Rainier and Princess Grace of Monaco to introduce Princess Caroline as a suitable partner a few years ago, but this came to nothing. When Charles met Caroline at the Variety Club gala in Monte Carlo in the early summer of 1977 he jested: "I've only met the girl once and they are trying to marry us off."

They water-skied, dined in some of the world's most elegant salons and generally tasted the delights of the Côte d'Azur, but eventually it became clear that nuptials were not what they or their families had in mind. The beautiful Princess returned to her sophisticated life among the stylish 'Tout Paris' – and an ill-fated marriage – while the Prince flew away to London to the more serious job of helping to organise his mother's Silver Jubilee celebrations.

There was always wide-spread speculation about Prince Charles and his girlfriends. But he was particularly discreet with anyone he really cared about and meetings took place well off the beaten track, sometimes in a trustworthy friend's house. He has a private retreat in the Scilly Isles for example, where he can relax away from the public eye.

One of his first romantic ties was when he met Lucia Santa Cruz, the stunning daughter of a former Chilean ambassador to Britain. Latin in temperament, very beautiful and feminine, but a clever historian with degrees from both London and Oxford universities, she was then the chief researcher on a book of Lord Butler's memoirs at Cambridge. Charles was completely fascinated by her for a time, but their friendship gradually waned, and their romance ended, but she was one of the most significant women in his life.

The American admiral's daughter, Laura Jo Watkins, who was briefly seen around with the Prince in 1974, was, according to some of his friends, brought on the scene to take the heat off that year's romance with Lady Jane Wellesley, daughter of the Duke of Wellington. Blonde and college-girl pretty, Laura Jo did not mind. She told the folks back home: "I had a fantastic time."

When Princess Anne became betrothed to Captain

Mark Phillips, a commoner, it brought Charles a double joy. One was because of the natural love he has for his sister, but the other pleasure came from the fact that his new brother-in-law did not come from the international royals. The acceptance of a commoner by the Royal Family, the Government and the people of Britain and the Commonwealth widened the choice available to Charles. He could decide on someone who had not been born to the sound of saluting guns.

Any girl from the ranks, however, would still have to be from a good family, well educated, and have an un-shakeable sense of duty. Knowing his taste in girls she would probably also have to be a good horsewoman, an excellent swimmer, enjoy an outdoor life, have an interest in music and a taste for adventure, and share his sense of humour. She did not have to be a classic beauty. She needed to be attractive and presentable rather than an absolute stunner. Her clothes would be in delicate good taste, not flamboyant, although he has never been noted for his awareness of what a girlfriend is wearing.

These qualities were what attracted the Prince to the blonde and lovely Davina Sheffield, the ex-debutante daughter of an army major. Davina and Charles first became involved with each other when Davina spent part of her summer holiday with the Royal Family at Balmoral. But four months later they broke up. Davina rather dramatically left London and headed for Vietnam, offering her services to international relief organisations. Because she had no nursing or medical training she could not get the sort of work she wanted to do among the sick and wounded. She did, however, find something worth-while to do. She looked after sixty abandoned or or-phaned youngsters in a rundown Saigon house. It was tough going, in miserable surroundings. When the Viet

Cong began to take over the country and infiltrate into the southern capital she hung on for as long as possible before fleeing to Thailand just days before the Communist take-over. She told friends in Saigon who were trying to persuade her to leave before it was too late: "I feel a real sense of purpose here and don't want to leave."

From Bangkok she went to Australia for a short while before returning to England and another meeting with Charles. Their mutual friends were delighted to see the two of them together again. He gave formal acknowledgment of his feelings for her by producing Davina in public once more as his glamorous and laughing companion during polo at Smith's Lawn, Windsor. During that long summer they spent more and more time together. Whenever he could get ashore from his naval duties he would be with Davina at some quiet country retreat, dining with just a few close friends, or having her meet his family again. Occasionally they would speed away in his 140-miles-per-hour Aston Martin Volante to what was once a secluded beach for surfing at Bantham, near Kingsbridge, Devon. For three months in 1976, while Charles was mostly at sea skippering a minesweeper, they did not see each other. But by September they were hand-in-hand again. Davina came from landed gentry stock and was a cousin of Lord McGowan. Vivacious, intelligent, warm and sensitive, with a ready wit, she was a suitably well brought up young 'gel', and fit for an English prince. Apart from the terrible scenes she witnessed in South East Asia, she also knew tragedy in her own life. Her widowed 62-year-old mother was murdered, battered to death, early in 1976 at the family mansion at Ramsden in Oxfordshire. Prince Charles' natural sympathy for anyone in distress was a great help

68

to her during the months she tried to get over her grief. But revelations about her past from an old boyfriend in a British Sunday newspaper dimmed the likelihood of her marriage to a prince.

There have been other young ladies besides Davina whose friendship Charles valued greatly, all of whom had impeccable pedigrees. Among them were Lady Henrietta Fitzroy, eldest daughter of the Duke of Grafton, whose mother was Mistress of the Robes to the Queen; Lady Charlotte Manners, daughter of the Duke of Rutland; fellow crazy-humour-lover Angela Nevill, whose parents Lord and Lady Rupert Nevill were close friends of the Queen; flaxen-haired Bettina Lindsay, offspring of a Tory politician, Lord Balniel; Georgina Russell, the elegantly beautiful daughter of British diplomat Sir John Russell – and of course, Lady Jane Wellesley.

For more than two years the pretty and petite only daughter of the most noble of families, the Duke and Duchess of Wellington, reigned supreme as the closest female companion of the Prince. They seemed so complete. She was always there waiting when he returned from the sea. Then, inexplicably, she suddenly faded from public view for about two years. During the summer of 1977 however, Lady Jane Wellesley and Charles became close friends again, reviving speculation that she might become a royal bride. But his friendship cooled off gradually and the rumours ceased.

These must have been very confusing as well as exciting years of romance for Charles. He allowed a glimpse of his bewilderment with his life as the great eligible bachelor at the time he was questioned about love on the day of the engagement to Diana. He answered, awkwardly: "What is love? Whatever love means, you can put your own interpretation." What love means to Lady Diana is that she expects him to take only her to his hideaway on the Scilly Isles from now on, and also perhaps that he disposes of the house he kept for the odd quiet engagement with friends. Lady Diana was among those he invited for dinners at this house in Campden Hill near London's Hyde Park not far from Princess Margaret's home. The existence of the hideaway in this area of expensive and fashionable early nineteenth century streets was a well-kept secret, even within the Royal Family: only a few members of Charles' most trusted circle, knew of it. The house was bought for the Prince's use at the beginning of 1980. It was certainly a perfect address as far as Lady Diana was concerned. Her eldest sister Lady Jane Fellowes lived just minutes away. Nothing was simpler for Lady Diana than to slip unnoticed up the road to the Prince's haven. The nearest pub was called, ironically, 'The Windsor Castle'.

Prince Charles had always insisted that he would not get married until he was around thirty, "after one has seen a great deal of life, met a large number of girls, fallen in love now and then, and one knows what it's all about." His sound, sane approach to love was always worthy of inclusion in a marriage-guidance pamphlet: "I feel an awful lot of people have got the wrong idea about what love is all about. I think it is more than just a rather romantic, glamorous idea about falling madly in love with somebody and having a love affair for the rest of your married life. I think it's much more than that. It's basically a very strong friendship. As often as not you have shared interests and ideas in common and also have a great deal of affection. I think where you are a very lucky person is when you find the person attractive in the *physical and* the mental sense. In many cases one falls madly in 'love' with somebody with whom you are in fact infatuated rather than in love. To me marriage, which may be for fifty years, seems to be one of the biggest and most responsible steps to be taken in one's life."

It was always almost certain that Charles would marry a Protestant, or someone willing to become one. This was because of a legal quirk imposed by George III, the eighteenth century monarch most historians have declared insane – though Charles disputes this verdict. George III forced through Parliament a piece of legislation which, more than 200 years later, was one of the major bonds in the straitjacket that prevented Prince Charles from marrying whomever he wished. George was annoyed because two of his sons married commoners. So he promulgated the *Royal Marriage Act*. Under this law Charles was in the hands of his mother and Parliament when it came to picking a bride. Lady Diana, a descendant of a long line of Protestants, fitted the bill perfectly. She would cause none of the fuss and bother of some of the foreign, but Roman Catholic, princesses with whom Charles' name had been linked. And he loved her.

71

Chapter Seven

ACTION MAN

Lady Diana had always known that she was taking in hand one helluva guy who enjoys risking his royal neck. According to one of her friends: "She knows it is going to be tough, but she loves him so much that she wants them to have not only a happy but long life together." Among the points that Diana and Charles discussed before the final decision to marry, were his daring Action Man–James Bond interests in risking his life. He has risked death at most activities that could possibly get the royal adrenalin flowing. And not all of them without nearly breaking his neck.

As a pilot in both the Royal Navy and Royal Air Force he has flown every type of aircraft from commando helicopters to over 1,000-miles-an-hour McDonnell Douglas F4 Phantom jet fighters. His first parachute jump during his RAF training nearly ended in disaster when he found himself descending towards the sea upside down with his legs caught in the rigging lines. Despite this, when he was made colonel-in-chief of the Parachute Regiment three years ago, he decided to carry out a full training programme with the other paras to earn his wings – and his lines got twisted again in one jump.

He has dived under the arctic ice, hunted for Russian

submarines as the skipper of a warship, and has now taken up the dangerous sport of steeple-chasing, the sort of gentleman's caper made world-famous by the death-defying Grand National at Liverpool every year which injures riders and often kills horses. He spends over £40,000 a year on keeping a stable of polo ponies – his greatest extravagance – and on at least two occasions he has been thrown so badly that he suffered injuries from being kicked by one of his horses, including a severe blow to the head.

Why does he do these things? According to Charles: "I always like pushing myself to the limit – just to see how far I can go. I get terrified at times." On another occasion the Prince has said: "I like to see if I can challenge myself to do something that is potentially hazardous, just to see if mentally I can accept that challenge and carry it out. I like to try all sorts of things because they appeal to me. I'm one of those people who doesn't like sitting and watching someone else doing something. I don't like going to the races to watch horses thundering up and down . . . I'd rather be riding the horses myself." This dislike of just sitting and watching is demonstrated to the limit when he is on official tours abroad. To him the World appears as a huge adventure playground, with a variety of people to meet and different ways of life to learn. His special position in society has made it easier for him than most other young men to try his hand at new and often daring experiences. A telephone call from the Palace could always fix most things, though much of his activities have been part of his training in the Royal Air Force and Royal Navy. He has been the envy of every schoolboy and a man admired by any adult who ever had Walter Mitty dreams. Queen Elizabeth, the Queen Mother, once said of her grandson: "If there was anything left to discover in the world, Charles would have been an explorer."

During an official visit to Canada, Charles was in the barren northern points of his mother's realm. He visited Resolute Bay in the Northwest Territories in April, 1975. He had been a sub-aqua swimmer for several years and could not resist joining a small band of divers who regularly plunged into the chillier parts of the Dominion. His experience included training to escape from submarines, so he was no stranger to climbing into a frogman's suit. Sinking beneath the Arctic ice, however, has always been only for the more daring marine brethren. He went under the ice with a Canadian scientist, Dr. Joe MacInnes, of Undersea Research Limited, who was trying to gain a greater understanding of both the surface and underwater aspects of life near the North Pole.

Charles remembered his dive as follows: "I lowered myself gingerly into the water, which by now was covered with newly formed pieces of ice – rather like *crème-de-menthe frappé* – and sank like a great orange walrus into the ice-covered world below. Once at the bottom of the six foot shaft, the similarity with a walrus vanished, and I found it extremely hard to preserve my balance and had to struggle to stay upright. Despite the rubber hood, the water felt decidedly cold around my mouth and a few other edges, not to mention the fact that with heavy gloves on my hands I could not get my fingers onto my mask in order to clear my ears. I thus 'ballasted' myself out at a depth which was not too painful and took stock of the situation. It was a fascinating eerie world of greyish-greenish light that met my gaze and above all was the roof of ice which disappeared into the distance. The visibility was extraordinarily good. Dr. MacInnes said the water was virtually silt-free due to the lack of wave action – the ambient light visibility was a hundred feet."

After the Prince got used to swimming around in the strange environment, occasionally using his hands to stop him from bumping his head against the underside of the ice pack, he decided to have some fun. Dr. MacInnes showed him how to do the upside-down walk on the underside of the ice and, he recalled, "I could not resist giving it a try! The result was comical in the extreme. I only partly succeeded. What was fascinating was to see the exhaust bubbles from the two of us trapped on the underside of the ice spread out like great pools of shimmering mercury."

His intrepid companion left Prince Charles floating around the craggy undersurface for a few minutes and dived to a shell-shaped station at the bottom of the sea. He returned with a bowler hat on his rubber-capped head and brandishing an umbrella. The royal frogman reached out a hand, took the umbrella from his scientist friend, and tried his hand at sub-aqua clowning. He opened the umbrella underwater and posed for pictures with Dr. MacInnes. Now that he was familiar with this jade-coloured underworld he decided to jolly-up the adventure a little more. He descended sixty feet to the shelter and entered it through an airlock with his fellow swimmer.

Inside he was shown some of the plants growing in a corner of the structure which was being used as a sea-bed laboratory. Then, switching to the surface listening post on the telephone link, Charles and the scientist sang The Beatles' song, 'We All Live In A Yellow Submarine'. The dive into this weird edge of the world lasted around thirty minutes. Forty minutes is considered to be the limit a first-time diver should stay in these scary conditions. It was a worrying time for the accompanying security men waiting nervously on the surface. No detective wanted to go down in history as the man who lost the future King of England – underwater.

When he made his 8,000 mile tour around the frozen Northwest Territories he sampled as much as he could of the land of the Eskimo. After he walked down the steps of his plane on to a remote airfield, clad in natty furskin, he was off for a ride on a dog sleigh. He soon got bored with being a passenger. Returning from a six mile trip over the snow and ice he asked his Eskimo dog handler to sit in the back and he took over the huskies.

Eskimo life fascinated Charles. He watched Eskimos fishing through the ice for seals. A short time later he came across more than he had bargained for, however, when he saw a demonstration of seal-skinning. A younger girl came up to him and offered the local 'delicacy' – raw seal meat. "I looked at it and said 'Ugh!' but she kept saying I must eat it," Charles remembers. "For the honour of the Family I picked up a piece of meat and made the fatal error, of course, of chewing it rather than swallowing it like a sheep's eye. The trouble was that it tasted absolutely appalling. I said 'The Press here are going to eat this and all the people with me . . . you'll all eat it.' They shrank away and disappeared. A doctor who was with us muttered in their ears that they shouldn't eat it because it was probably a week old. So I said 'Thank you very much chummy, what about me? Eh?!'"

Due to his amazing attraction to dangerous sports Prince Charles has suffered many an injury and ailment. But he always goes back for more. From an early age, Charles sported bumps and bruises resulting from the rough and tumble of tough physical activity. When he was seventeen he broke his nose while playing an over-enthusiastic game of rugby at his public school. He was later put out of action again with a bout of pneumonia after an adventure camping holiday with his school friends. June 1972 found him sporting an embarrassing look due to a sticking plaster covering a graze on his chin. He got in the way of a fast-moving polo ball during a practice game.

In 1980 Prince Charles suffered several mishaps while playing polo. In April he was rushed to hospital in Florida after he nearly fainted from heat exhaustion and fatigue while playing at Palm Beach. Back in England, he has taken several tumbles including being thrown by his pony and kicked in the face. And that's not counting the four falls he's had in a dangerous cocktail of fox-hunting and steeple-chasing called 'eventing'.

His polo handicap was recently raised from three to four, putting him within reach of international class. Only seven other British players rank higher in the sport. (In polo, unlike golf, the higher the handicap the better.) Diana is not as keen on horses as Charles and other members of his family, but it looks like she is going to have to show more interest – just like any other new wife whose husband is sports crazy. Charles once said: "I love the game, I love the ponies and I love the exercise. It's my favourite game." He has played it all over the world, including India, from where the game was brought to Europe by the officers of the British Raj in the nineteenth century.

Charles has been playing polo since he was sixteen and keeps a string of ponies at Windsor. He learned to ride ten years earlier on a small Shetland pony he used gently to trot across Windsor Great Park, where he now gallops. He mounted up for his first chukka while he was at

Gordonstoun School. His father captained a team of novices, including Charles, who had the excitement of scoring a goal in his very first outing. One of the regular players with Charles says: "He is absolutely fearless. He is very aggressive and thunders along at a frightening pace. Over the past ten years he has become a player of top international class." This frightening pace may account for his recent run of tumbles. And he hasn't escaped them all lightly. The most serious was when he was thrown and trampled in a practice game and ended up with a hoof-shaped bruise near his heart and the cut that required nine stitches near his left ear.

But until his marriage plans were announced at least, he had even more spectacular plans for himself. Having ridden in a flat race at Plumpton and over the fences in National Hunt racing at Sandown, he fancied his chances in the Grand National. He has told organisers at Liverpool that he would like a shot at the world's toughest race but the Queen is understood to be against the idea saying: "That's enough, Charles!" Whether or not he'll take heed of her or his new wife is yet to be seen, but certainly there will come the day when he must accept that enough is absolutely and utterly enough, and opt at last for more sedate pastimes. Until then Diana can only hold her breath every time he leaps out of a plane, gallops across the polo ground, dives under the polar ice-cap or goes mountain climbing.

It looks likely that his keen horsemanship will continue and Diana will have to sit at the sidelines and worry alongside her mother-in-law. But jumping out of aircraft and diving under polar ice-caps are probably over for good. It is going to be hard for Charles to accept, but with children more than likely on the way within a few years, he is going to have to become a responsible family man.

He will never be the boring middle-aged pipe-and-slippers sort – but the parachute has more than likely been hung up forever. With the lovely Diana to distract him it's not going to be too much of a sacrifice.

Chapter Eight

AIR FORCE AND NAVY DAYS

Prince Charles' love of danger and adventure, his wish "to appreciate life that much more and to really want to live it to the fullest" have perhaps been most clearly shown in his time serving in the Royal Navy and Royal Air Force.

Prince Charles joined the RAF at twenty-three. He went to Cranwell, the Air Force College in Lincolnshire which has been the training ground for top pilots for nearly fifty years. He was able to jump the queue somewhat in the Royal Air Force and only had to go through a streamlined, speeded-up course. As a graduate qualified pilot, he was gazetted as a Flight Lieutenant before he set foot in the college. He carried the rings of rank on the sleeves of his uniform as he flew to Cranwell to be inducted into the service. With understandable ostentation, he piloted himself there in a twin-engine, Bassett light aircraft of the Queen's Flight. Waiting for him, apart from a line-up of top RAF brass, was a five-month programme which would bring out in him that excellence needed to qualify for wings in the Royal Air Force. The senior officers who greeted him made it clear that he was going to have to earn his wings. A true case of 'per ardua ad astra' – through hardship to the stars.

The operation to get the royal pilot to supersonic level

was code-named 'Exercise Golden Eagle'. He became part of the first course made up entirely of university graduates, sharing a flat with three other ex-student cadets and, like them, he was subject to Service discipline. Heading towards the stratosphere was Charles' ambition, but before he was allowed to go aloft in one of the two specially maintained Provost jet trainers, he had to go through a gruelling test on the ground. He was locked in a decompression chamber, 'taken up' to 20,000 feet in simulated conditions – then ordered to unhook his oxygen mask. The effect of this is just like the moment before blacking out in the dentist's chair, after being given a whiff of anaesthetic. A pilot becomes drowsy and loses his bearings before feeling himself disappear into a void. Charles had to experience this in the testing chamber so he would recognise the symptoms if his oxygen supply went wrong while he was in the air. During this oxygen training at an aero-medical training centre not far from Cranwell he had to leave his mask off for several minutes and do simple handwriting tests until he was on the verge of blackout. What he wrote during his highly uncomfortable experiment is rumoured to be in language appropriate to the discomfort of the time. It is a choice piece of memorabilia which the RAF has tucked safely away for historical purposes.

Although it was not his wish, the Air Force went to incredible lengths to make sure Charles got through his flying course safely. Radar kept his aircraft under constant surveillance when he was flying, and other aircraft for fifty miles around Cranwell were ordered to keep clear. A maintenance team twice the usual size made sure that the two 480-miles-per-hour Provost trainers, earmarked for him, were always in faultless condition. In addition his planes had special red flashing lights fitted to distinguish them from other trainers. The Junior Service did its best, but the Prince presented them with a major problem that only he could solve. One of the essential qualities for any pilot is a ready understanding of mathematics. Charles, unfortunately, has always been towards the bottom of the class when it came to mental arithmetic and rapid calculation in such pastimes as algebraic equations, geometric fomulae and logarithmic tables, a blind spot he shares with the Queen. As he is the first to admit: "Maths taken in its pure context is misery I think. I find it boring. I'm one of those people who prefers ideas rather than numbers. I could never understand maths. I always thought it was the way I'd been taught originally that made me so hopeless, but, on the other hand, perhaps I just don't have a mathematical mind."

Prince royal or not, a pilot without some skill in mathematics was of no use to the Royal Air Force. He just had to get up to scratch. He put his head down and, fighting his way through a battlefield of unfriendly figures, managed to reach a maths standard that satisfied his instructors. Even today though, he says with remarkable honesty: "From the flying point of view my arithmetic is not as fast as some other people's." Once in the cockpit of a jet trainer, with the controls in his hands, the natural talent he has above zero feet flashed through. He quickly got the hang of flying jets and was soon learning the aerobatics needed by a jet-age fighter pilot. He made his first solo flight after only eight hours' instruction instead of the usual ten. Just a few weeks after he had gone solo, Charles co-piloted an F4 Phantom of Forty-three – 'The Fighting Cocks' squadron from Leuchars in Scotland. He took part in a scramble and an interception over the North Sea with another Phantom acting as 'the 'enemy', then his aircraft nudged in carefully behind a Victor tanker to take on 1,200 gallons of fuel – one of the hairiest of airborne manoeuvres. Few pilots like doing this because of the risks of an explosive collision. He flew as high as 40,000 feet and as low as 1,000 feet when he made a pass over Balmoral in a final flourish. When he landed he was made a member of the exclusive Ten Ton Club, that enviable group who have piloted a plane at more than 1,000 miles per hour.

The next day he sat in a more spacious cockpit, alongside the captain of a Nimrod NATO maritime reconnaissance aircraft, for a day-long patrol over the Atlantic. For four hours he piloted this four-engined jet whose main function is the detection, and in wartime, the destruction of submarines. With sophisticated radar and underwater search equipment, just one Nimrod can monitor the surface and undersea movements of the entire Mediterranean in a few high-flying minutes. The Prince then rounded off his tropospheric education a week later in a nuclear bomber. He co-piloted a Vulcan, the delta-wing aircraft that is the mainstay of the British strategic strike force. With four powerful engines it travels at just under the speed of sound with a frightening destructive capability of either missiles, hydrogen bombs or 21,000 pounds worth of what are chillingly called 'conventional' bombs. The citizens of Doncaster, an industrial town in the North of England, were not aware of it at the time, but they had the privilege of being the target when their future king made a high-level dummy attack on them.

For his helicopter training, Charles joined the aptly named Red Dragon flight of Number 707 naval squadron at Yeovilton in Somerset. He was trained to handle one of the most difficult aircraft to fly, the big Sikorsky S-58

Westland helicopters. For three and a half months he worked hard at getting the hang of controlling and navigating a Westland in all weathers and over any type of terrain. Mountain flying was the most difficult and the most hazardous. He did this among the peaks of his own principality of Wales, actually landing on top of its highest peak Mount Snowdon. He trained in air-sea rescue work, learning to manoeuvre just above wave tops, blinded by the spray his own rotors were throwing up, in order to winch volunteers to safety from the water. Charles was also taught how to fire weapons such as rockets and guided missiles, and how to take commandos into battle.

After 105 flying hours, spread over forty-five days, he went solo and qualified as an operational helicopter combat pilot – ready for anything, anywhere in the world. Red Dragon flight became a front line squadron on board the commando carrier HMS *Hermes*. Charles and the rest of the newly trained pilots were taken to the other side of the Atlantic. They flew in the sub-tropical temperatures of the Caribbean and below zero in Northern Canada. Helicopter flying became the greatest thrill of his life. He said at the time: "It's very challenging. There's that superb mixture of fear and enjoyment which comes over me. It is marvellous when things are going right and you can pick up a reference on the ground and not bother with the map. Then that panic when you don't really know where you are and you've got to sort it out yourself. It's so exciting. I've given myself a fright or two. The other day we were going along quite well when flames suddenly started to shoot out of the engine on my side, making extraordinary whoof-whoof noises. All the instruments were twitching away. Fortunately, I was with the senior pilot of the squadron so we shut down the engine and landed in a ploughed field beside a motor-way, much to everybody's amazement!"

During his RAF training, Charles made a parachute jump from a twin-engined Andover of the RAF Support Command over the English Channel, down to a bay on the Dorset coast. When the plane was in position, at an altitude of 1,200 feet, a sliding door opened near the tail and the whistle of the slipstream could be heard. Below, the sea looked a long way down. The despatcher nodded to Prince Charles that he should get ready and walk to the edge of the heaving doorway. He stood up, steadying himself to get his balance. The static line that would, hopefully, pull out his 'chute as he left the plane was attached to a cable. He checked his reserve 'chute, strapped on the front of his blue flying overalls, and the quick release catch. The despatcher, Flight Sergeant Ken Kidd, thought he was a little too far from the door, and suggested a few steps forward might be in order.

With less than a minute to go the Andover began its final run over Studland Bay, a holiday beach near Poole, in the area of the English coast which launched the D-Day Invasion of Normandy. The Prince gripped the side of the exit. A green light went on and Kidd tapped him on the shoulder and shouted "Go!". Charles jumped without hesitation. With a welcome jerk the Prince felt the canopy open, but then something went wrong and he found himself descending with his legs caught in the rigging. He kept his cool as he dropped towards splash-down and later recounted the incident objectively: "I determined to myself that I wouldn't think about the jump too much beforehand. Otherwise I would have worried. In the end I stood in the doorway and I didn't need kicking out. I jumped out happily except that after I'd jumped, for some unknown reason – I must have hollow legs or something – my legs went over my head. The next thing I knew they were tangled in the rigging lines, so I was looking up at them and coming down in a sort of U-shape. I said to myself calmly, 'Your legs are in the rigging so you must remove them.' So I removed them – fortunately – by about 800 feet. Then I had a lovely sail down to sea level. Of course I forgot to inflate my life jacket because I'd enjoyed it so much." When he hit the sea, motor launches, manned by Royal Marines, fished him out of the water within ten seconds and whisked him away for a stiff drink.

In the years since he gained his pilot's licence, Charles, both a civilian pilot and a service flyer in the Royal Air Force and the Royal Navy, has flown everything from a helicopter to a jet bomber. Like every pilot who has had to face up to the final terrifying test of going solo, Prince Charles remembers that moment well. "It's imprinted on my mind indelibly. I suppose I worried about it for a bit . . . the thought of actually having to go solo and whether I was capable of doing it. Whether I'd remember the right things to do. But when the day came, the instructor got out of the cockpit, rather surprisingly as I didn't think I was going to do it that day, and said, 'Right – it's your turn!' So I sat there with butterflies in my tummy while he got out and then when I was actually airborne I was amazed how much more fun it was. I flew round and round and admired the scenery. I controlled my butterflies. Then I did a perfect landing as it turned out – I never did a better one after that."

From that day onwards, just like his father, flying had got into his blood. He could not get enough of it and a spell in the RAF was inevitable. When Charles, or any member of the Royal Family, goes flying, either by helicopter or in fixed wing aircraft, they travel in the most carefully monitored airspace in the world, just like Air Force One. They are given a flight path exclusive to themselves and no other aircraft is allowed to enter or cross it.

"Treat 'em mean and keep 'em keen," about sums up the hardy old seadog philosophy of Britannia Royal Naval College, Dartmouth – the British Annapolis. It is a view of life shared by the officers on the staff who deal out a formidable amount of that meanness. Britannia, or the Stone Frigate as she has been called by generations of naval officers who have suffered on her parade ground, lies among the flower beds and green acres alongside the River Dart in an otherwise delightful part of Devon in Britain's West Country. Its primary task is to train and lick into shape the successors to Admiral Nelson. It has been the unofficial finishing school for future British Kings for almost a century. Prince Charles' ancestors all had to go through it. His father, Prince Philip, his grandfather, George VI, his great-grandfather, George V and his great-great-grandfather, Edward VII. All had the final touches of royal lustre painfully varnished on them there. Young Charles had to brace up to it in his turn. On one occasion towards the end of his career at sea he said: "I feel that if one is going to get involved in the whole spectrum of life in this country, then one should get to know about the Services. One should get to know about the Navy particularly because ultimately our security and everything depends upon the Navy. It always has done throughout history and always will. Therefore it is very important to know about it. Having learned at school that discipline exists, and I'm highly disciplined myself, it helped me in the Navy."

Charles went to Dartmouth in the late summer of 1971 to prepare himself for the five years he was to spend as a Royal Navy officer in what will one day be his King's Navy, to learn at every level from bridge to lower deck the operations and the cherished legends of Britain's Senior Service. He had already served at the Royal Air Force College, Cranwell, won his wings and graduated from Cambridge University with a Bachelor of Arts degree. Because of these qualifications he did not have to join the Navy as an ordinary cadet. Acting as a sub-lieutenant the Prince of Wales was among a dozen university graduate officers who 'went aboard' Britannia to take a crammed six-week course before going into various branches of the Royal Navy. He had a twelve-hour non-stop day from early morning until dusk. Before seven each morning his steward Joseph Atkinson woke him up with just enough time to reach breakfast in the sub-lieutenants' mess. Mr. Atkinson kept the Prince's cabin tidy, but the young officer had to polish his own shoes and keep his own clothes and uniforms smart. With just a short time available, the instructors tried to make the Prince and his classmates worthy of command. On the parade ground there were three hour-long sessions each week in addition to the daily parades, including marching, standing to attention, saluting, and, even in the age of nuclear submarines, sword drill. None of Her Majesty's officers is expected to survive without eighteenth century sword drill! In the gymnasium there were at least two hour-long sessions every week, planned, according to one of the sports officers, "so that one reaches the limit of one's endurance in a very short space of time." For his first swimming test, Charles had to swim four hundred metres in a boiler suit, float for three minutes, then dive to the bottom of the college pool and pick up a brick eight feet down. He also learned life saving and how to give mouth-to-mouth resuscitation on a blonde Swedish dummy known to the cadets as 'Resusci-Anne'.

But most of the busy days were spent in classrooms learning the text-book techniques of life at sea, and studying navigation, weaponry, marine and electrical engineering, administration and management. This sort of training certainly puts this prince a cut above the rest. It was rough going, but in the end Prince Charles got through his first major test as a naval officer. Under a peevishly dull sky on the last Friday of October in 1971 he and his fellow graduate officers led the passing out parade of 500 officer cadets while the band played, appropriately, 'God Bless the Prince of Wales'.

The Royal Navy was a career that Charles enjoyed, although a profession he was allowed to follow for only a brief time because of the other demands of apprentice kingship. Thanks to the family tradition the Royal Navy meant a great deal: its history of smoke, cannon and valour interested him. The rewards of serving in it excited him and gave the Navy a chance to get to know him. He had the opportunity to meet his future subjects at close hand. There were few secrets in some of the tiny ships he served in. He got used to living at close quarters with everyone from the jolly old chaps out of the well-bred households that have traditionally supplied Britain's officer class, to the occasionally fruity-tongued 'Jack' whose mum and dad might live in tenements. "You're all together out there at sea, in that small community, cut off," the Prince once said. "It's a very intense, communal life." He soon got the hang of getting on with the seamen he commanded. After five weeks at sea in his first ship, the guided missile destroyer, HMS

Norfolk, he came ashore at Portsmouth Dockyard for a few days' leave. A rating who, like the rest of the 400-odd men on board, had been watching closely the way the newcomer found his sea legs said: "The lads like him. He listens to you . . . you don't think of him as Royalty," and added "He's a good shipmate!" The 'good shipmate' also showed he could mix-in socially with the best of them when he went to the Norfolk's annual dance, an occasion very special to the crew, a big night out ashore with all their wives and girlfriends. Wearing his sub-lieutenant's uniform, he danced with the wives of fellow officers and ratings and dipped his hand into his pocket to pay for his share of drinks. The three years following that marching-out parade at Dartmouth were mainly spent at sea, in a great variety of ships, learning the profession of being a naval officer, in all parts of the world. He gained his watch-keeping certificate – the Royal Navy's 'driving licence' – during the nine months he was on the *Norfolk*. This qualified him to be in complete charge of a ship, responsible for every decision he ordered as officer-of-the-watch on the bridge.

During these three years, and all his time at sea, he was spared none of the duties the other officers had to carry out. Yet, at the same time, he still had his royal functions. He had to study State papers, stored in specially secured safes in his various cabins, keep up with the administration of his estates and handle the usual heavy load of royal correspondence. While other officers could relax in the wardroom, he caught up with briefings on State affairs, read reports and recommendations from his staff at Buckingham Palace or the London offices of his estates and decided on the hundreds of requests received every year from all nature of organisations and societies for his royal patronage and support.

Charles managed to collect a sea-bag full of happy memories and adventures on board HMS *Jupiter*, his fourth ship. He went half-way round the world in this 2,450 ton frigate, flying first to join her in the Far East, then sailing across the Pacific to the West Coast of America, and through the Panama Canal for the return Atlantic journey to Britain. For much of the four months on board he was the radio officer, but he also took his turn on the bridge, taking the responsibility of watch-keeping. He was not long out from Singapore one stormy day in the South Java Sea when he helped to rescue the twelve-man crew of a tug in distress. While he was manning the bridge the radio room picked up S.O.S. signals from the stricken Singapore tug *Mediator*, which had gone aground in the storm. Prince Charles ordered a change of course to the scene and alerted the skipper, Commander John Gunning, who joined him on the bridge. The captain backed the young officer's decision and sent off the ship's tiny Wasp helicopter on a search sortie in the driving rain. The pilot, Lieutenant Lawrence Hopkins, spotted the tug and its two barges being battered in the foul weather. It needed seven airborne attempts to put a boarding party on the tug and barges with towing lines. Then, after four hours of dangerous, touch-work in fiery conditions *Jupiter* and her men freed the vessel and pulled them to a safe anchorage. Such was the anonymity of Charles as just another officer doing his job that it is doubtful even today that those twelve men realise what royal hand came to their rescue.

By this time he had been promoted – he was now lieutenant Charles Windsor. The crew had, however, given the Prince of Wales another name – 'Taffy Windsor' – noting the usual first name of a Welshman, 'Taffy'. When *Jupiter* reached the other side of the Pacific and was taking part in exercises with the United States Navy in California's San Diego Bay, the Welsh lieutenant saved the ship from what could have been a disastrous collision with another warship. He was navigating officer, keeping a close watch on the radar in thick fog, when he spotted the blip of the other ship on the screen heading straight towards *Jupiter*. The other vessel was the USS *Grindley*, more than twice the size and weight of the British vessel. Charles flashed off urgent signals and, with hasty manoeuvring, the two missed each other by forty feet.

Charles spent five years in the Royal Navy, until he reached the level of being the captain of his own ship. In the New Year of 1976 he was eventually given his own command, after studying at the Navy's senior 'university', the Royal Naval College, Greenwich. With Britain's small navy of today there are few ships of any size around to put in the hands of a prince. In the end Charles became the skipper of one of the smallest ships in the fleet, HMS *Bronington*. The 360-ton *Bronington* – named after a Welsh village – is a wooden-hulled mine-hunter. When Charles joined her she had such a bad reputation for unsteadiness because of her flat bottom that she was said to "roll on wet grass". Her nickname in the service was 'Old Quarter-past-eleven' – her pennant number was 1115. During his ten months on board he often had great difficulty controlling the ship in even the slightest hint of bad weather. She became the only ship in his entire naval career to make him seasick, a malady he could claim to have shared with Nelson. She was so tough to handle that when he docked her at Rosyth after his first ten weeks at sea as skipper he said: "They took ten years off my life . . . I feel about eighty."

The *Bronington* was a workhorse, given the tasks that

the larger vessels could not be bothered with. Charles took her minehunting, and blew up the odd mine. For two days he shadowed a Russian submarine caught prowling around Britain's coast and North Sea oil rigs. He zig-zagged among the supertankers and large cargo vessels passing through the world's busiest – and riskiest – seaway, the Straits of Dover. He was there to check on 'rogue' skippers who were not keeping to the navigation rules. He took part in NATO exercises, bringing his 36-man crew to battle stations against mock attacks by 'Russian ships'.

Charles, with his sense of humour and fine skill at getting on with people, was a popular skipper. When he gave up his command at the end of 1976 he had a rousing send-off from his shipmates. They hung a black polished lavatory seat round his neck with 'HMS *Bronington*' inscribed on it in gold letters, to remind him of the weight of the throne! It is still one of his most treasured possessions, and one that Lady Diana, Princess of Wales, is going to have to get used to as a reminder of her husband's more boisterous past – afloat.

Chapter Nine

THAT PRINCELY STYLE

As he approaches marriage Charles is a well-rounded man. His main hobbies and interests are not just polo, surfing, underwater diving, flying, but also music, art, history, and archaeology. He enjoys listening to and playing music. His tastes are mainly for the classical. His favourite composers are Bach, Mozart and Berlioz. He has a passing interest in jazz and rarely bothers about pop. He used to be a fan of The Beatles because he thought they had an exceptional talent both as musicians and lyricists – "the more I heard of them the more I enjoyed them." He used to play the trumpet and the piano, but without great success. Then one evening he went to The London Festival Hall for a performance by the cellist Jacqueline du Pré and was so impressed by the rich deep sound, that he decided to take up the instrument himself.

In art he prefers the paintings of the seventeenth and eighteenth centuries. He enjoys Rembrandt and Van Dyck and also likes Rubens. He does not have much of an eye for modernists, especially Picasso, whom he regards with distaste. He is an artist of no mean skill himself. When he first tried his hand at water-colouring he was taught by the notable Norfolk artist, Edward Seago. His reading is mainly non-fiction with only the occasional novel. Generally, he tends to read history and biographies. He is particularly fond of the theatre and enjoys almost any sort of play, comedies, thrillers, musicals, or the classics such as Shakespeare and Ibsen. London, with justification, is to Charles the greatest theatrical capital in the world. Given a choice, he goes for comedies.

On the question of food, he prefers plain English cooking but also enjoys good French cuisine. Charles likes a solid breakfast, and for lunch or supper, grilled meats, fish and salads. He is not too keen on sauces. One of his favourite desserts is a good portion of creme caramel. His favourite comedy show was *The Goons*, starring the late Peter Sellers and up to the time of the comedian's death he often used to meet Peter Sellers and try to impersonate his mad antics. Royal Sellers craziness livened up what was becoming a very stuffy and formal evening when Charles visited the Royal Regiment of Wales for the traditional St. David's Day celebrations in the officers' mess. The Prince, as their Colonel-in-Chief, had called on them when they were stationed at Osnabruck in West Germany. As a newcomer to the mess, he had to follow the custom of eating a raw leek and then burst into song. Instead of singing something very regimental such as 'Rule Britannia' or very Welsh, like 'Land of my Fathers', he chose a gibberish song made famous by Sellers. Keeping a very straight face, he shook the diners into laughter with the 'Ying-Tong' song, a constant repetition of the verse: 'Ying-Tong, Ying-Tong, Ying-Tong, Ying-Tong Tiddle-I-Po'.

Much of his humour involves poking fun at himself. When he was at Cambridge, he quite happily sat in a dustbin in a student theatre sketch about the dustman who used to wake him up every morning by noisily collecting the rubbish beneath his window. In another sketch, written by himself, he came on stage underneath an umbrella and informed the audience: "I lead a sheltered life." For one production he volunteered to sit patiently on stage while he was bombarded with custard pies in the old Laurel and Hardy slapstick tradition. "I love imitating and mimicking," he says. "I enjoyed acting enormously at school and university. In a strange way, so much of what one does I find requires acting ability one way or another, and I enjoy it. For instance, if you are making a speech it is extremely useful if you can use acting techniques, I mean timing and *double entendres* and everything are enormously helpful. I enjoy making people laugh if I can and I always believe humour is a very useful agent towards getting people to listen to what you are saying."

His speeches show a brand of wit that clearly demonstrates he has a streak in him that forbids pomposity and stuffiness about his role in society. Just before he took over as Captain of the *Bronington* he told a gathering of the show business fraternity, the Grand Order of the Water Rats: "If any of you here are considering sailing on the North Seas next year, or you happen to own an oil rig in Scottish waters, I strongly advise you to increase your insurance contribution forthwith." Unveiling a bust of Prince Philip, he commented: "This does not mean that I am accustomed in any way to unveiling busts," and, as the drapes fell away, he added, "I now complete the process of helping my father to expose himself."

Humour in speeches he explains thus: "I've thought about it from my own experience. When I'm listening to someone else talking, if I get bored because they are not being amusing or something, my eyes glaze over and I'm not paying attention. I think about something else or go to sleep. When I see that glazed look coming over my audiences, that's the time to leap in and punch with something funny if you can. They wake up again and you can start again with the serious stuff." He has an acute sense of what is ridiculous. When he flew back from training with the Royal Marines in Canada to be invested as Great Master of the Order of the Bath, he commented to his then secretary, David Checketts: "What I find amusing is that I come back after three weeks under canvas to become the Great Master of the Order of The Bath. Rather appropriate I would say."

Practical jokes are also part of his comedy armoury. At Cambridge he often introduced himself as "Lord of the Isles" or "Charlie Chester", justified, he thought, because he was, after all, Charles, Earl of Chester. He once went out to bat during a charity cricket match mounted on a pony and carrying a polo stick. When everyone was wearing name tags at a Royal Air Force dinner Charles wrote on his label: "Watch this space." He pulled a fast one on a group of American photographers when he was on board *Jupiter* and she docked at San Diego. The pressmen were at the quayside trying to get pictures of the Prince. They asked the officer of the day to persuade Charles to come up on deck and pose for them. The young Royal Navy Lieutenant told them: "You're wasting your time, he's very pompous and not a very likeable chap you know. He isn't very bright, either, by the way. I'm quite sure he will not meet you, so you'd better go away and save your time." The cameramen walked away grumbling without realising they had, in fact, been talking to their prey. The impishness of his character helped to cheer up the barrack rooms of the Royal Regiment of Wales after that visit to share leeks with them in Osnabruck. Some of the soldiers grumbled that, because they did not speak any German, they were having trouble meeting the local girls. Charles promised them he would try to do something about their problem, and a few days later, sent them two light-hearted sheets of German-English phrases which he and his secretary had compiled with a vocabulary limited to the pursuit of women.

He likes to drive his sports car fast but takes great pride in believing that he is a skilled and careful driver. He never takes risks and is annoyed by people who do. Charles is not one for discotheques, with their decibel-shattering noise, smoke and crowds. In the Navy, however, he would have boisterous runs ashore with his fellow officers. In Caracas he stayed until four o'clock in the morning in a nightclub with what Charles described as "a party of beautiful Venezuelan ladies". He also recalled: "As the ship sailed at six-thirty that morning I was not in a good condition at all." A perfect evening for him used to be to take a pretty girl to the theatre followed by a quiet supper either at Buckingham Palace or in the corner of a discreet restaurant. He likes parties but he doesn't drink much. He always says that he can get 'drunk' on the atmosphere alone. At a party he tries to make everyone relaxed, to put them at ease, and make them accept him as just one of the gang.

Charles is not fussy about formality when he is relaxing with friends and acquaintances. On one occasion an elderly knight who was entertaining him asked: "Would you like a drink, sir." The Prince blushed and his host thought he had offended him by offering alcohol, but Charles explained: "I'm not used to being called 'sir'". He has a very few close friends he trusts completely, certain that they will not let him down by spreading gossip about him or telling any tales about his behaviour when he lets his hair down in private. Despite the friends, Charles until now led a fairly solitary existence. "In a sense, one is alone, and the older I get the more alone I become," he once said.

At Buckingham Palace Charles has a three-roomed flatlet cut off from the rest of the building on the second floor. It is decorated in pale colours and furnished in a leathery masculine style. The bookshelves contain mainly volumes on history, archaeology and art. Other shelves have his collection of Eskimo soap-carvings including one of a huge musk-ox. On other shelves are eighteenth century *objets d'art*, bought with the help of a friend who searches around the London salesrooms for him. The Prince was always a bit fussy about keeping the place neat and tidy. He is apt to get annoyed over clutter. Charles has enormous drive and tremendous energy to carry out whatever he has committed himself to. He is a phenomenally hard worker. If he agrees to become a patron of some organisation or get involved in a scheme to promote something British he doesn't accept the job until he is sure he can join in wholeheartedly. It might be charity work or a group to promote products from Wales, yet he hammers away at each task tirelessly. As he says: "I don't believe in having totally honorary positions. If people expect me to become a president or patron and just sit back they've got another think coming. I like trying my hand at things and if somebody says do you want to have a go I usually say 'yes'." His involvement goes down to the smallest detail. As Colonel-in-Chief of the Royal Regiment of Wales, for example, he wants to know whenever any of the regiment's soldiers are wounded on service in Northern Ireland. He sends them a large bottle of whisky with a cheery get-well message.

It is customary for most royal speeches to be researched and written by staff at Buckingham Palace. The Queen or Prince Philip then put the odd final touches to them. Charles writes his own speeches, expecting help from his staff only on the research. He is always reluctant to express any controversial views in public because he suspects that once they are recorded they take on a permanency that can become embarrassing for him in the future. His presence, he has learned, produces extreme reactions from some people. They either behave obsequiously, almost grovelling at his feet, or they effect an air of pointed indifference. Charles considers the first to be unnecessary, while the latter verges on rudeness, especially when he tries to be friendly at all times with strangers.

"People always say to me, 'How boring it must be to have to meet so many people all the time?' I always say 'absolutely not' because I find that one of the greatest advantages of my position is that I can meet all the most interesting and fascinating people in the world. I can learn a great deal – I always think one of the most important things in life is to be a good listener. I'm quite happily prepared to do the talking if nobody else is going to, but otherwise I find it very enjoyable indeed to pick somebody's brains and to really find out about their experiences." He once summed up his lifestyle this way: "I do quite as much of what I like to do as is good for me, and I do quite a lot of things which are work, just as everybody else has to work."

He likes people to approach him, but he understands the difficulties of breaking down the barriers: "Unfortunately the nicest people are those who won't come up and make themselves known. They're terrified of being seen to be friendly in case they'll be accused of sucking up to me and because they imagine, quite wrongly, that I won't want to talk to them. I used to think 'Good God, what's wrong? Do I smell? Have I forgotten to change my socks?' I realise now that I have to make a bit of the running and show that I am a reasonable human being. An awful lot of people say eventually: 'Good Lord, you're not nearly as pompous as I thought you were going to be.'"

He has great energy for work and usually gets through the programme of the day with the precision of a Swiss watch. He rehearses speeches with care and allows for passages where he expects people to laugh. When he stands in front of the microphone he is word perfect. Out of courtesy to her position he never refers to "my mother" in a speech, always to 'The Queen'. He is usually more informal as far as Prince Philip is concerned and frequently calls him 'my father'. If there is an official programme he doesn't want it altered – unless it is his decision. Calls for impromptu speeches, or switches in arrangements made without warning by local officials, do not please him. As he flies around his mother's world-wide dominions, Charles is very wary about getting involved in local politics. Before a visit the advance party, or the local embassy, assesses any sticky problems he might face. He gets a run-down on the topics to keep clear of and any person to be on his guard against.

No matter where he is in the world, Charles has to keep up with bags of duty mail that are flown in regularly. He sends his replies, like all the members of the Royal Family, on special thick paper called 'Original Turkey Mill Kent'. If it is a personal letter he often hand-writes himself, but usually one of the secretaries who travel with him types his answers. They bear no stamp, but are marked with the royal insignia on the back and on the front with the letter 'E.R.', Elizabeth Rex.

Charles has to show interest, no matter how often he may have witnessed familiar fancy footwork in countless halls and arenas and heard so many conventional orations. He stays bright, alert, and inquisitive for two reasons. One is that questing spirit to know about everyone and everything, while the other is the natural development of his royal training. A close friend of the Royal Household said of this aspect of Charles' life: "If you've been brought up to feel it's your duty to be interested in everything and everybody, after a while it's second nature to you."

Charles has never been inclined to become a leader of fashion. Sober, conventional clothes have always been his cut. He seems to follow the advice given a hundred years ago by the Prince Consort, to his great-great-grandfather, Edward, Prince of Wales: "A gentleman will borrow nothing from the fashion of the groom or the gamekeeper." He shies away from flamboyancy and prefers the discreet good taste of the well-pressed Saville Row area. His suits are made by Hawes and Curtis where his personal tailor is the doyen of wardrobe good taste, Mr. Edward Watson. Charles orders his shirts by the dozen and ties by the half-dozen from Turnbull and Asser, the renowned blue-cottoned firm in St James's where the world's most stylish fellows clad themselves.

He seems to have met everyone from cannibals to astronauts, from charladies to film stars and his easy manner has made friends of them all. During his tour of America towards the end of Jubilee Year he could be seen cracking jokes and holding his own in the razzmatazz of some of Hollywood's big names; he even managed to steal the limelight from superstar Farah Fawcett-Majors of TV series 'Charlies' Angels' fame when he met her. Charles also enjoyed a trip round the film studios, indulging his curiosity and his love of comedy by watching the shooting of the 'M.A.S.H.' series. The ordinary citizens of San Francisco were as impressed as the film stars with Prince Charles' ready smile and friendly quips, when he took a ride on one of their famous cable cars; earlier on that trip, visiting San Antonio in Texas, he was besieged by a crowd of admirers who almost pulled him off his feet in their enthusiasm. Texas provided another exciting experience when he tried his hand at cattle-driving on the ranch of Mrs. Anne Armstrong, the former United States ambassador in London. He really saw some action when, with the guidance of Mrs. Armstrong's husband Tobin, he was shown how to rope and herd several hundred steers. Visiting Hollywood and Texas, Alaska and New Guinea is the glamorous, fun side of Charles' job, but the other, more serious aspects of his future are always at the back of his mind and for him they are just as exciting.

Chapter Ten

HIS DIFFICULT CHOICE

Charles always knew that the girl he would choose as his queen would have to be a rare creature. Well bred enough to understand her place and the place of others in England's complex class structure, resilient enough to project a brave face to the world while under stress. His future bride had to be charming, elegant, worldly, caring, motherly, beautifully groomed and above all learn all the attributes of stateswomanship, tact and diplomacy needed to be the woman behind the king. Charles also realised full well that his position was vastly different from that of his sister. Anne could marry a commoner because she was not immediate heir to the throne. He was in a unique position. He could consider a commoner, but regal traditions made such a choice more difficult for him. On one of the many occasions when he was asked about the girl he would marry, the Prince answered: "This is awfully difficult because you have to remember that when you marry in my position you are going to marry someone who perhaps one day is going to be Queen. I've got to choose somebody very carefully, I think, who could fill this particular role and it has got to be somebody pretty special. I often feel I would like to marry somebody English or perhaps Welsh. Well, British anyway."

The age of the arranged marriage has passed, how-ever. Such has been the affection among the British people for their Royal Family that his future subjects would only want Charles to marry a woman he truly loved, who would give him the strength of a happy home life and support him with her affection while he carries out the onerous duties of Kingship. Diana, Charles has obviously discovered, fits the bill, but despite all his girl friends, he was always under severe restrictions. George III's Royal Marriage Act of 1772 meant that Charles, as heir in direct line to Mad George's father, was in the hands of his mother and Parliament when it came to picking a bride. He could not simply take the girl round for tea one Sunday afternoon to meet the family. He had to satisfy the requirements of the Queen, the House of Lords and the House of Commons. Until the age of twenty-five he could only marry with the consent of the Queen. If she had refused permission, he could still ask for the approval of both Houses of Parliament. Had the Queen turned down his choice it seemed highly unlikely that, even in this democratic age, the Lords and the Commons would approve of the match if the girl was so eminently unsuitable to be formally rejected by Her Majesty.

George's parchment of marital mischief was just one of several archaic laws that held in check Charles' rights as a suitor. The only regal legislation that did not seem to apply to him was the Statute of Treasons passed in 1351 which fussed over the chastity of ladies royal and prom-ised the chopping block or gallows for any over-amorous seducer of princesses. The greatest barriers to his free-dom were the Acts governing not only the religion – but even the colour of his bride-to-be. Under an Act of 1689 she had to be a white Anglo-Saxon Protestant, so there would have been as much concern if he cast his eyes towards a Negress, Arab or Asian, as if he had fallen for a Roman Catholic. The famous – or infamous – Bill of Rights also demanded that Charles declared himself an 'enemy of the Catholic religion'. Needless to say, it was passed at a time of great religious intolerance in England. With its intentions, however, according to some experts, it ruled out a Roman Catholic changing her religion, or merely agreeing to have the children brought up according to the teachings of the Church of England. To make the path of love even harder, this Act made it quite clear that he would lose his crown if he married a 'papist'.

This risk to his throne was made still clearer in the Act of Succession of 1701, the law from which Charles would be given the legal authority to rule. This Act invokes the out-dated Bill of Rights as the source for its insistence that he should forfeit his crown by marrying a Roman Catholic. To enable Charles to have a Roman Catholic Queen, Parliament would have needed to pass new laws either repealing the earlier Acts altogether or at least amending those passages which would seem offensive to a large percentage of the non-protestant population of Britain and the Commonwealth. A future Queen who was Roman Catholic, therefore, looked out of the question, unless Charles contemplated abdication. He takes the role of continuing the royal lineage of the House of Windsor so seriously, and regards his own part in the destiny of his family so highly, however, that abandoning the throne for love was never part of his character. If he had so drastically followed the example of his great uncle, the Duke of Windsor, and put love before the throne it would probably have endangered the British monarchy altogether. Two abdications in forty years could have jeopardised the monarchical system in Britain forever.

Because of the very responsible attitude he has to his duties as heir, all the speculation during 1977 about a betrothal to twenty-three year old Roman Catholic Princess Marie-Astrid of Luxembourg eventually angered him, although he always took an amused view of speculation on his marriage prospects. Every few months a new name kept popping up in the world's gossip columns, some of them girls he has been genuinely fond of, but many he hardly knew. He greeted most of this speculation with wry amusement and when the gossip about his romantic associations got a little too out of hand he took it in his stride. He once shrugged his shoulders and said, in the manner of a much slandered film star: "The time to get anxious, in a way, is when nobody's interested at all." The 'Astrid Affair' as it became known at Buckingham Palace, was too much, however, and it raised his hackles in a most untypical way. One reason was that he had never even contemplated marrying her. He had met Marie-Astrid on only three occasions and he could not remember these clearly. Despite this, gossip columnists at home and abroad persisted in linking pretty, fair-haired 'Asty', as she became known, with Charles. Hadn't the Queen and Prince Philip visited her father and mother the Grand Duke and Grand Duchess in Luxembourg? Then the Grand Duke popped over to Sandringham for a spot of shooting with Prince Philip.

The Grand Duke had, after all, been educated at one of Britain's leading Roman Catholic public schools, Ampleforth, in Yorkshire. During the Second World War he became a private in the Irish Guards carrying out sentry duties at Buckingham Palace. Surely he qualified as the perfect father of a future Queen of the United Kingdom?

Charles, himself, had said: "The one advantage of marrying a princess, for instance, or somebody from a Royal Family, is that they know what happens." Surely, said the gossip writers, that was significant. Then Marie-Astrid went to Cambridge to take an English language course. More gossip. She was also a direct descendant of Charles the First of England. Talks between Roman Catholic and Church of England representatives over the sticky matter of religious difficulties were reported to have taken place. Experts on the delicate subtleties of royal accession were called in to give their opinion that Astrid need not renounce her Catholicism. Girl children of the marriage could remain attached to Rome while boys could satisfy the Church of England by becoming Protestant. Should girls-only be the result of the proposed 'union' then the line of succession could pass to Charles' younger brother Prince Andrew – hopefully with a spouse who was a fine upstanding Protestant.

Despite denials from Buckingham Palace about any romance, the rumour continued. When the gossip and rumour-mongering reached its peak four years ago, Charles ordered the Queen's Press Secretary at the time, Ronald Allison, to put out an official denial of any romance with Marie-Astrid. Charles told an acquaintance later: "What could I do throughout the entire period of these rumours? I'm sure Marie-Astrid is a marvellous young woman, but I hardly know her. At the same time it would have been highly discourteous of me to start putting out denials while the talk was merely gossip. This could have been interpreted by some as me saying publicly that a European princess was not good enough for me. I didn't want to offend her and I thought the whole business was highly amusing until things became too much."

During the week that the denial was issued he still kept tongues wagging by being seen with two perfectly eligible young ladies: Lady Camilla Fane, daughter of the Earl of Westmorland . . . and Lady Sarah Spencer.

Chapter Eleven

THE PRINCE DECIDES

Diana drove home from her kindergarten and prepared for the evening of 6 February 1981 with special care. She chose a long evening gown for what was to be the most important night of her life. This time there was no long motorway drive. The rendezvous was very close, hardly enough distance to warm up the engine of her Mini Metro. No one noticed her slip away from the mansion block in the Old Brompton Road clutching a small evening bag, a warm coat round her shoulders. The policeman in the green Buckingham Palace security post at the big wrought iron gate nearest to Green Park waved her straight through. He had been warned to expect the red Metro at 8 p.m. and Lady Diana was spot on time. She drove through an archway into a small quadrangle where her distinctive car would be hidden from the view of the railings at the front. A footman opened the door to the billiard room entrance but Lady Diana didn't need to be shown the way to the small apartment at one corner of the huge Palace, for she had been to Prince Charles' private rooms as a guest before that night.

The Prince of Wales, formally dressed in a dark suit, was waiting for her in the small plainly furnished sitting room of the three-roomed bachelor flat overlooking the Mall he had occupied since the age of twenty-one. A small round table was set for supper with a white linen cloth, silver cutlery, a bowl of flowers and a single candlestick. Charles and Diana sat side by side on a small satin covered sofa chatting and making small talk about his skiing trip, anything that came to mind. They had missed each other and there was a lot of news to catch up on. Diana later told friends that the Prince seemed very nervous; perhaps at the last minute he was having second thoughts. After all, a marriage by the heir to the throne was a marriage for life, and there could be no turning back, no divorce. He was about to take that momentous step, losing his bachelor's freedom. He was bound to have butterflies in his stomach. Diana too felt terribly nervous. As she told her father afterwards, she was so frightened and excited at the same time that the evening passed in an odd dreamy way as if she wasn't actually there at all. It was as if she were standing back watching another girl sitting at that beautifully laid supper table.

A servant had lit the single candle and served a simple meal ending with cheese and fruit, but later Diana couldn't recall what they ate at all. Over the flattering candlelight the Prince popped the question. The actual words will remain their secret but after the "will you" Charles gave Diana time to think. He didn't expect an answer immediately, he expected her at least to say that she wanted to go away and give it some thought and was a little taken aback when the blonde teenager, her blue eyes sparkling in the flickering candlelight said 'yes'. He had given her time to think about it all and she had already made up her mind long before the night of 6 February that she was deeply in love with the Prince and wanted to be his bride. They kissed and talked and talked about their future, about their plans and their hopes.

There was an awful lot of planning to do and the single candle on the uncleared supper table had almost burned out by the time Diana drove home.

Prince Charles went about the business of planning his forthcoming marriage in a very old fashioned, very proper manner. The proposal had been romantic and perfect and he was going to make sure that he did everything else in a gentlemanly manner too. First he went to see his own parents to tell them the good news. The Queen and Prince Philip were both delighted. The Queen had already told other members of the Royal Family that Lady Diana, who of course she had known as a child, was a 'perfectly delightful young lady', and after Diana had joined them at Sandringham the Queen had made it quite clear that she thought the teenager would make a perfect bride for her eldest son. Then in the proper English manner Prince Charles had to ask Diana's father for his formal consent. Etiquette specifies that the Prince should have gone to see the 57-year-old Earl Spencer at his home. A romantic novelist would have put the two men in armchairs over a glass of port with the Earl asking "Now young man what are your intentions?" In fact it didn't work out like that at all. Charles made a slightly more modern approach to ask for the lady's hand in marriage. He used the telephone.

The Earl answered the phone at his London flat just across from the American Embassy in Grosvenor Square. Prince Charles called the Earl "Sir" with a nice old fashioned touch and the two men laughed over the slightly ludicrous situation as the Prince formally asked the question that the Earl had expected since Christmas. "Over Christmas I realised Diana was in love," said the Earl after the Prince told him: "I would like to marry your daughter, Diana, who much to my astonishment, has

Lady Diana sitting alone in the grounds of the kindergarten, 1980.

Above: Lady Diana pushing a pram when working at the Young England kindergarten, 1980.

Opposite: Lady Diana with two of her charges at the kindergarten, September 1980.

Above: Lady Diana at Sandown races to watch Prince Charles ride in the Military Gold Cup.

Opposite: Prince Charles with Lady Diana and the Queen Mother in the paddock at Sandown Park, March 13th, 1981.

Above: Lady Diana before the engagement, 1981.

Opposite: Lady Diana and Prince Charles at their first public function together, attending a concert at Goldsmiths' Hall, London, 1981.

An official engagement picture.

already said 'yes'." Later the Earl, who has a fine sense of fun said: "I wonder what the Prince would have said if I had told him 'no'. In fact I told him what he already knew, that Diana was a wonderful girl and that he was a very lucky man." Like an excited schoolboy the Earl rushed off to tell his wife, Diana's stepmother, Raine, who had also spotted, with a touch of woman's intuition, that Diana was in love with the Prince. The Spencers, like any other couple, wanted to tell everyone about the engagement, but couldn't. The few people who were to be told that day were sworn to secrecy for the next three weeks.

Diana had asked for some breathing space before being hurled into the searching spotlight which would be turned on her the moment the official announcement was made, and more importantly, like any other young girl contemplating marriage, especially such a marriage, she wanted to talk to her mother. Mrs. Frances Shand-Kydd was in Australia, holidaying at her husband's sheep farm in New South Wales and Diana needed to see her and not just tell her the news over a long-distance telephone call. That week-end must have been an extraordinarily difficult time for the excited nineteen-year-old. She had told her father and her mother but she ought not to tell anyone else and she was bursting to. She really shouldn't have told her best friends, her flatmates, but what young girl could keep such a secret to herself? The fact that none of the three girls breathed a word during the next three weeks showed the great strength of friendship between all four girls. Any one of them could have made a fortune by selling the information to the papers.

She did it very quietly and with no fuss just before she packed her bags to join her mother in Australia. Ann Bolton remembered later that Diana walked into the

113

kitchen and said simply "I'm engaged". The noise of Ann and Virginia Pitman screaming with excitement in the kitchen was heard by nineteen-year-old Carolyn Pride while she was in the bathroom, and it was left to Lady Diana to tell her flatmate the news through the closed door. "We knew how much in love the two were," said Ann after the world knew about the engagement. "But when she told us about the engagement it completely threw us. We started running all over the place, laughing and shouting. Diana just sat there giggling at our antics, clearly thrilled by it all." The four girls who had all been friends since their schooldays popped the cork on a bottle of champagne to celebrate – even Diana, who doesn't normally drink, had some. None of the girls had ever met Prince Charles, but they were to be honoured guests at the wedding and were to meet the man who had been just a voice on the telephone. Keeping the secret during the next three weeks was to be a terrible strain for these three flatmates, but somehow they managed not to tell a soul.

Diana packed her bag, told them where she was going, and left for the airport on Sunday. She flew from Heathrow on Qantas flight QF2, first-class to Sydney. She expected to be seen, but amazingly was not recognised until she arrived in Australia where she was met by her mother and rushed off to the privacy of the farm. Before long of course the farm was turned into a sort of mini-Sandringham, ringed by reporters and photographers, Australians, not Britons this time, searching for the elusive Diana. One newspaper even hired a helicopter to circle the farm in the hope of seeing "this sheila" as the Aussies called her. Protectively, Mrs. Shand-Kydd tried to get rid of the press. She even resorted to outright lies, not an easy task with all that scrutiny, by telling the pressmen: "My daughter is not here. You have got the wrong continent. She is in the sun somewhere, but not here." Not entirely convinced, the pressmen gradually drifted away and Diana was able to relax, even going out to a beach for the day, hidden behind dark glasses and a headscarf, to picnic and sunbathe. Mother and daughter had a long chat. Diana did not need to be told what sort of responsibility would rest on her young shoulders but she did need her mother's counsel.

Since Diana's arrival the phone had never stopped ringing, mostly with calls from the press, the usual reply to any of the callers was "Diana is not here" but two days after her arrival one male caller was more persistent than most, "I am the Prince of Wales," he said. "Oh yeah, how do I know?" said the farmhand who had answered the phone. "No, look I really am," said the Prince of Wales making an early morning call from Buckingham Palace. The tough Australian was not impressed and eventually Charles had to ring another number before he was connected to his fiancée. Charles has a strong romantic nature and didn't forget to make another call to his sweetheart, on 14 February, St Valentine's Day, and this time he was put straight through to her. Diana had been sending postcards to her father and to her friends at Coleherne Court, but she had given no indication of when she was returning home. Meanwhile, with Diana out of Britain, the hungry press corps had to content themselves with taking pictures of Prince Charles carrying out his official duties.

Her return to Britain was planned with the precision of a military attack. Charles realised that the attention of the press would be distracted by an event taking place on 19 February, so it would be an ideal day for Diana to come home. 19 February was his brother Andrew's twenty-first birthday. The lad himself was currently training as a helicopter pilot at the Royal Naval Station at Culdrose in Cornwall nearly 300 miles from London. Quite rightly, Charles realised that the group of pressmen who were assigned to sniff out his romance with Diana would be sent down to Cornwall to try to find out what Andrew was doing on his birthday. Sure enough the pressmen set off for Cornwall just as Lady Diana boarded a Qantas flight home. She slipped through Heathrow Airport unnoticed and went into London to pick up her car. She even popped into Harrods but, unfortunately, this was her downfall. Although her picture had appeared hundreds of times in the papers Diana was not instantly recognisable, especially dressed in a coat and silk head-scarf like hundreds of other girls who live and work in the Knightsbridge area. But one person did recognise her, and she had a friend on one of the papers.

Diana drove down to Highgrove for her reunion with her husband-to-be. They were full of joy, happy to be with each other again little knowing the heartbreak and tears that day, 20 February, would bring. The previous night the flickering light from the log fire had sparkled back from a spectacular ring. Charles had taken the large oval sapphire surrounded by fourteen perfect diamonds and set in eighteen-carat white gold from a small blue velvet lined box and slipped it on the third finger of Diana's left hand. It fitted perfectly. Before she flew to Australia, Diana had picked out the design she wanted from a catalogue delivered to Buckingham Palace by Garrards the exclusive Royal jewellers. A man from the discreet shop went to the Palace to measure Diana's finger. He didn't have to be sworn to secrecy, it would never have occurred to him to tell anyone. Garrards have been used by the Royal Family for generations. Even

116

after the engagement was announced the jewellers refused to say how much the Prince paid for his fiancée's ring. More than £30,000 is the closest speculation can go. A similar ring is on offer in the Garrards brochure for £28,500. Diana's ring, a rush special job, would probably have cost more.

On this bitterly cold morning of 20 February the Prince and the future Princess of Wales threw caution to the winds. Diana wasn't wearing the ring, but it was safely in her handbag in its presentation box. Charles decided to drive to Lambourne to ride his racehorse Allibar on the Downs. The following day he was to ride the animal over the jumps at Chepstow racecourse in the fourth race of his hopeful part-time career as a jockey. Diana sat in the front passenger seat of his blue Ford for the fifty mile drive to Lambourne, Berkshire. It was something she had never done before. In the past they had always driven separately. Wrapped up in their joy over seeing each other again the Prince had relaxed his guard against the press just once, and he almost lost the game. As they drove unhurriedly along the M4 motorway to Lambourne the press were speeding up behind them. The night before word of the sighting in Harrods had reached the Royal press gang, who like to call themselves 'The Mafia' as they were futilely searching the pubs of Cornwall for birthday boy Andrew. It was obvious to them that Diana would go straight to Charles at Highgrove. It was a long drive from the Cornish peninsula to Berkshire and 'The Mafia' set their alarm clocks for three a.m. Arthur Edwards, a burly Cockney who had been chasing Prince Charles for most of his career as a photographer on the *Sun* newspaper, was dozing in the front seat of the fast Jaguar limousine being driven by reporter Harry Arnold.

There weren't many vehicles on the motorway at that time in the morning and Arthur looked up as they overtook a blue Ford that looked familiar. Prince Charles, the driver, looked back at Arthur in horror. Arthur couldn't believe his eyes, for there beside the Prince in the front passenger seat was Lady Diana. Fortunately for the Prince and unfortunately for Arthur his camera bag was safely locked in the boot of Harry's car. As the duo from the *Sun* peered at the Royal driver and his companion the police intervened. A back-up car, a powerful Rover with a V8 supercharged engine containing two armed Special Branch men who had been tailing the Royal car, swept up behind the *Sun* 'Jag', ordering them to pull over with flashing headlamps and waving hand signals from the two worried policemen. Harry put his foot down and the faster Jaguar outpaced the police. This cat-and-mouse game continued for several miles. During this time Charles was trying to work out how to avoid Lady Diana being photographed, as he didn't want his carefully laid precautions against the press to be wrecked now, only days before the engagement announcement. Using his usual short cut through the back of a deserted service area the Prince lost the newspaper men in the lanes leading to the riding stables. Diana went straight to the Downs, which are private property and out of bounds even to newspapermen, while the Prince stayed at the stables saddling up Allibar for what turned out to be a tragic last ride.

The Prince was besotted with the magnificent horse which he had bought the previous year. It was his dream to ride the animal to victory in a big prestigious Grand Military Gold Cup race at Sandown Park on 13 March. The race at Chepstow was just a warm up for that day. With a wave to the *Sun* team who were left without their snaps of Lady Di, as they called her, the Prince wearing a black crash helmet rode Allibar up on to the Downs for a seven-mile canter. The Prince had finished the seven miles and was just trotting up to where his sweetheart was standing on the edge of the downs when Allibar started jerking convulsively under him. Charles, realising that something was wrong, quickly dismounted. He had only just stepped clear when the huge eleven-year-old suddenly crashed to the ground. Horrified, Diana, who had watched the whole thing, dashed over. The Prince was on his knees, his arms round the animal's neck trying to comfort it, but it was too late, Allibar was dead. The Prince was heartbroken, and Diana who shared his love for the superb looking animal, burst into tears. Stable lads who were exercising other mounts on the Downs watched in amazement as the couple stood with their arms round each other beside the dead horse. The Prince, white faced with shock and red eyed, was trying to comfort his fiancée as the tears rolled down her face. It was more than ten minutes before they were able to pull themselves together enough to drive off to the home of the Prince's racing trainer, Nick Gaselee.

Twenty-four hours later a veterinary surgeon's post mortem report on Allibar revealed that the horse had died of a massive heart attack. There would have been no warning and the coronary could have happened at any time. If the horse had crashed to the ground during the next day's race at Chepstow the result could have been very different. The Prince could have been badly injured, even killed, if the horse had rolled over with him still in the saddle. Diana, her eye make-up ruined and her face streaked with tears, did not want the waiting photographers to see her looking like that, so with the help of the two detectives and the Gaselee family a new escape plan was put into operation. A mud-splattered grubby Land Rover was driven up to the side door of the cottage and Diana was bundled into the back covered with an old horse blanket just as if she were a criminal emerging from a courtroom. The Land Rover sped off followed by the Prince in his Ford. The policemen in the brown Rover blocked the lane, effectively stopping the press party who now numbered six, from giving chase. It certainly was no way to treat a lady but, in the circumstances her departure was hardly surprising. The couple had planned to spend the week-end at Highgrove, but with their discovery by the press and the tragic death of Allibar their happiness had been somewhat tarnished. Diana went back to London and Coleherne Court on that Saturday morning, leaving the Prince to go hunting with the Beaufort in Gloucestershire.

The Prince and Diana were to meet again on Saturday night at a formal gathering of the Royal clan. Nearly all the senior members of the Royal Family were present for the dinner at Windsor Castle. They included the Queen, the Duke of Edinburgh, the Queen Mother, Prince Andrew, Princess Anne and Captain Mark Phillips and Princess Alexandra. Diana went into dinner on the arm of Prince Charles. She was the guest of honour that night as the final decision was made for the date to announce the Royal engagement. The dinner had originally been planned to celebrate Prince Andrew's birthday but it turned out to be a far more important gathering. On Sunday she told her flatmates that the date for the announcement had been fixed. It would be the following Tuesday at eleven a.m. Over the week-end Buckingham Palace told quite a number of people that Tuesday was the day. Prime Minister Mrs. Thatcher, her staff at

Number 10, Downing Street, and some of her top cabinet ministers were informed, and so was the Archbishop of Canterbury, Dr. Robert Runcie, the man who would perform the marriage ceremony and a message was sent out, under great secrecy, to the heads of the British Commonwealth all over the world.

In Fleet Street rumours started to spread on Monday afternoon. Calls were made to Buckingham Palace Press Officers who refused to reveal any information. That afternoon Lady Diana left her flat carrying a small suitcase containing the clothes that the world would see the next day, a red velvet outfit with matching red stockings and shoes and a vivid blue two piece suit which she had bought in the ladies dress department at Harrods. At five p.m. she drove to Buckingham Palace where she was spotted and photographed by a freelance cameraman who, with the click of a shutter, made himself a small fortune. Later that evening Lady Diana moved into the little room which was to be her home for the next few months, the spare bedroom at Clarence House, just 500 yards from Buckingham Palace. Clarence House is the home of the Queen Mother who had readily agreed to make Lady Diana her guest.

24 February 1981 dawned cold but bright with even a touch of sunshine to brighten up a drab London. The eleven a.m. announcement from Buckingham Palace, which was now common knowledge in Fleet Street and Whitehall and the subsequently touching interview with the happy couple would brighten the lives of millions that day. Diana was up early. This was her first day in her new role as a future fully fledged member of the Royal Family. Her life had completely changed. There would be no more driving round London by herself in her little red car. She would never be completely alone again. The

night before she had been introduced to the armed detective who would now discreetly accompany her everywhere, Chief Inspector Paul Officer, aged forty. Officer was a close friend of the Prince as well as his bodyguard. He had protected the Prince for the last twelve years and had saved him from an attack by a mentally disturbed naval officer who had burst into the Prince's quarters.

This morning at eight-thirty a.m. he drove her in the Prince's blue estate car to (where else?) the hairdressers. Diana had made an appointment with the same South Kensington establishment which had been doing her hair for five years. Owner Kevin Shanley, aged 25, who is also hairdresser to Lady Diana's two sisters, stood in amazement as Diana walked in and waved her huge diamond and sapphire engagement ring under his nose. "What do you think of that?" she said. "We all stood round in amazement and wished her the best." Kevin and his staff were given a real head start on the news, the first 'outsiders' to be told of the forthcoming marriage. Her thick blonde hair washed and set, Lady Diana was driven to the Palace by her new policeman. It was the start of a momentous and exhausting day for the teenage girl.

At exactly eleven a.m. the Buckingham Palace Press office released a simple, somewhat terse message, which was flashed round the world:

"It is with the greatest pleasure that the Queen and the Duke of Edinburgh announce the betrothal of their beloved son the Prince of Wales to the Lady Diana Spencer, daughter of the Earl Spencer and the Honourable Mrs. Shand-Kydd."

Chapter Twelve

WHAT A DAY!

Their joy was plain to see: in their eyes, in the way they touched and in the laughter they shared. "Blissfully happy" were the words Diana used, the light sparkling like champagne from her spectacular sapphire and diamond ring. "With Prince Charles beside me I can't go wrong," said the lovely teenager who was telling the world how she would become Princess of Wales and one day Queen of England. On the steps at the back of Buckingham Palace leading down from a stone flagged terrace which overlooked lovely ornate gardens and a lake, Diana rested her head for a moment against the Prince's neck in a gesture of pure affection. He placed his hands on the shoulders of her vivid blue pure silk suit and they laughed and laughed. High spirited, like a schoolgirl, Lady Diana revealed that she had answered the Royal marriage proposal "straight away".

Diana and her Prince were pouring their hearts out to the world's press whom they had spent the last six months so studiously avoiding. The time was around noon on 24 February and everything was going perfectly. Earlier, sitting side by side on the sofa in the same sitting room where the Prince had asked for her hand in marriage, the couple had given an interview which would enter the history books as one of the frankest ever given by a member of the Royal Family. Then Diana and Charles had undergone an ordeal by television. Two tough TV reporters had grilled them about love and even the twelve-year gap in their ages. The unsophisticated teenager, totally unused, unlike her fiancé, to public appearances had come out as a winner. It was the endless smile of pure happiness on the girl's face that really said what words couldn't and delighted the 500 million viewers round the world who watched that five minute interview.

Prince Charles took the lead as they were interviewed with Lady Diana laughing quietly and at first playing purely a secondary role.

How did they feel?

"Absolutely delighted and frankly amazed that Diana is prepared to take me on," said Prince Charles jocularly.

"Absolutely delighted too, blissfully happy," said Lady Diana.

Lady Diana was asked when they first met. "I first met him in November 1977. Prince Charles came as a friend of my sister Sarah for a shoot. I never saw Prince Charles before 1977. I was always paired with Prince Andrew." Here she gave one of her nervous giggles.

When did they decide to get engaged? Prince Charles: "It was about three weeks ago, believe it or not, just before Diana went to Australia. She planned to go to Australia quite a long time before anyway and I thought I will ask her then so she will have a chance to think it over so she could say 'I can't bear the whole idea' or not, but she actually accepted."

Lady Diana (with a giggle): "Straight away . . . There were quite a lot of telephone calls."

Prince Charles: "So many telephone calls from the press in Australia saying they were Buckingham Palace

124

or me. When I called, the man said 'How do I know who you are?' I said 'Well you don,'t, but I am,' in a rage. It was quite difficult to keep the secret for three weeks but we managed it."

The wedding date? Prince Charles: "No date as such, but certainly the idea is the latter part of July which is probably the easiest from all sorts of peoples' points of view. We haven't actually fixed the date." He added: "It is much nicer to get married in summer."

The BBC man asked if he might dare ask about the honeymoon. "You can dare," said Prince Charles. "We don't know. There is a lot to be decided and worked out."

Where would they live after the wedding? Prince Charles: "Basically, I hope, down at Highgrove in Gloucestershire. I dare say that that means we will have to try and find somewhere in London to have as a base as well, but at the moment Highgrove. There's an awful lot to be done there . . . marvellous to have someone to take it on, organise everything, because it's completely empty at the moment – I'm just camping out – and there's a great deal to be done isn't there?"

Lady Diana, again with a small laugh, agreed: "Yes."

Asked about being in the public eye, foreign travel and public engagements, Lady Diana said: "Naturally quite daunting, but I hope it won't be too difficult."

Prince Charles said: "I am very much looking forward to meeting lots of different people," and a laughing Lady Diana said: "I am going to have to."

Prince Charles: "When I first started public engagements, I think about the same age really, twenty, it wasn't easy to begin with obviously, but after a bit you do get used to it. You just have to take the plunge. I hope I can help pass on the bit of experience I have."

He turned to Lady Diana and said: "You like people which is a great thing."

What about their age difference – he is thirty-one, she is nineteen. "Never really thought about it," said Lady Diana confidently.

"I haven't, I mean, it's only twelve years," said Prince Charles. "Lots of people have got married with that sort of age difference. I always feel you are as old as you think or feel you are. I think Diana will keep me young. That's a very good thing. I shall be exhausted."

After the TV technicians, the still photographers and the reporters had packed up and driven away from the Palace, delighted by what they had in their tape recordings and film cans, the future Princess of Wales found herself in a very strange new world. She would never be able to wander out and have her hair done again as she had earlier that day. She would never be able to pop down to the shops, especially the little late night supermarket she was particularly fond of near her flat, where she would buy her breakfast grapefruit and milk. Worst of all she would never be able to enjoy cosy evenings with her friends left behind at Coleherne Court.

That evening for the first time Lady Diana and Charles were able to get in the same car together without fear of being spotted. It was the end of months of secret meetings in country estates with high walls and long drives. They were able to proclaim their love for everyone to see. Diana had changed into a full length skirt and a simple gown, her Prince was in an evening jacket and bow tie and Diana was still flashing that stunning ring she was so proud of. It was only a 500 yard drive to Diana's new home at Clarence House, there to have dinner with the Queen Mother and her Lady-in-Waiting,

Lady Fermoy, who is Diana's grandmother. It was a wonderfully relaxed evening after a day that had gone off so perfectly. Diana was even trying out a sort of regal wave for the first time, smiling and turning to a group of elderly women royalists who had braved the cold to stand outside Clarence House singing 'Congratulations and Jubilations' to the tune of a once popular hit song by Cliff Richard. It was a fairytale way for a Prince to announce that he had found his lady at last.

The announcement of their wedding brought the vital news of joy that Britain, and perhaps the world, needed at a time of gloom. President Reagan and British Prime Minister, Margaret Thatcher, were just about to meet in Washington for the first time to discuss problems that spread from massive unemployment not only in their own countries, but throughout the world. Armaments, more tanks, more troops, higher defence budgets were being talked about both in Washington, London and Moscow. Détente was not working out – and new men both in Moscow and Washington were deciding on how they would face up to each other. For the superpowers there was trouble spreading from Afghanistan to South America, via Middle East tension and Far Eastern chaos. And for the people relying on the world leaders to sort out the mess, the main task each day was finding enough work and money either to buy gas for the car or a loaf of bread, depending on which hemisphere they lived. In Britain a potentially disastrous miners' strike was at hand. Then, at eleven o'clock on a spring-like morning enormous joy was brought into the world with a handsome young couple holding hands and hugging each other on the green lawns of a huge private house in the centre of London. Sure there were more matters of import to face the world – but here, at last, was joy. A reminder to everyone, no matter what religion, political view or regime that love still existed. There was still cause for happiness. President Reagan and his wife, Nancy, heard the news on TV over breakfast in the White House. "Ronnie and I are absolutely delighted," said the First Lady. "I have never met Lady Diana but I have met her stepmother and I know they are a marvellous family."

Canadian Premier Pierre Trudeau said, according to a spokesman, "Everybody is pleased, excited and elated."

The rumours had been going the rounds of Britain's newspaper capital, for at least six months, but, when, at last, they could burst forth, the editorials let fly with the joy that reflected the reaction of most of the nation. The traditionalist *Daily Express*, which has always been a defender of the Commonwealth and royalty opinioned robustly under the headline 'ROYAL RAY OF SUNSHINE – It may have been the worst kept secret in the world, but nothing will detract from the delight which the whole nation will share with the Royal Family on the engagement of Prince Charles to Lady Diana Spencer. His Royal Highness could not have made a better choice for a future Queen of England. She is British through and through and from a family of historical distinction and numerous royal links . . . A royal engagement and a summer wedding could not have come at a better time. The mundane facts of British life at the moment are pretty grim. The dreary statistics of unemployment and falling production, strikes and threats of strikes, have depressed us far too long. What better than a royal romance to warm and cheer all our hearts? All the world loves a love story and this is the premier love story of the decade. It will be the occasion of a genuine national celebration, and who will say that we do not need one?'

Another royalist and traditionalist publication, the *Daily Mail* remarked 'Some Princes do have all the luck' then commented: 'At last, it is to be royal wedding bells. And we are delighted for them both. Prince Charles is a very lucky man. He has played the field and led the ladies a merry dance. And now he has been accepted by a lovely girl, who still has the freshness of the morning dew. Ah well, what's the point in being Prince of Wales if he can't do that? Dull of heart, indeed, must the citizen be who does not share in the happiness of Prince Charles and Lady Diana. Yesterday the whole nation seemed to be smiling.'

The *Daily Mirror* said: 'Now we can look forward to a summer wedding. The bride will be radiant, the brides-maids beautiful, the mothers tearful, the Prince, charming, of course. And on the day we'll all forget our problems for a while. Hopefully the sun will shine and even if it doesn't, who will care? We'll celebrate a splen-did British occasion: a Royal marriage. The greatest show on earth.'

The ultra-respectable *Economist* said: 'The Monarchy is the main British institution that still works, chiefly be-cause the British have learned when, and when not, to take it too seriously. While foreign republicans have to rally in moments of patriotic emotion round heads of state who – nearly half the population may be simul-taneously shrieking – should be sent to prison for burg-ling Watergate or accepting diamonds from a cannibal chief, the British entrust the unifying role in national policy to a family supposed to derive its authority as head of British morality from its inalienable birthright . . .' Then, referring to that great authority on not only British but world-wide monarchies, it went on: 'Debrett has discovered that Lady Diana Spencer descends five times from King Charles II, although four times from the wrong side of the blanket; but the real point is that British monarchy works well because its blue blood is constantly diluted by charm and fun.'

There had to be at least one sour note, of course, and this came from the Communist *Morning Star* whose main circulation is beyond the Iron Curtain. In what, one hopes, was a tongue-in-cheek article it reported under the headline 'DON'T DO IT LADY DIANA': 'Lady Diana Spencer is to sacrifice her independence to a domineering layabout for the sake of a few lousy foreign holidays. As the future Queen of England she can expect a fair bit of first class travel and a lot of attention, but with a £100,000 home of her own and a steady job as an exclusive nursery nurse, who needs it?' It could not have pleased the *Morning Star* editorialists later that day either when the capitalist trading on the London Stock Exchange went up a few points with news of the engagement and the pound strengthened on the international money markets. Obviously everyone loves lovers – even Zurich bankers. And in the same way that what is good for General Motors is supposed to be good for America, the prospect of a royal wedding was obviously good for Britain.

On the London stock market there was a rush to buy shares in firms likely to cash in on the rush for souvenirs or in the hotel business. Shares which had been sluggish the day before leapt dramatically. Hopes that the celebrations would pull in more American tourists boosted the shares of hotels group Trust House Forte by 7p to 200p a share. China manufacturers Royal Worcester, famous for their commemorative plates and mugs, jumped 23p a share to 293p. Pottery and tableware group Wedgwood also put on 5p, while Birmingham Mint, famous for commemorative silver and gold medallions, jumped 17p to 223p. Mr. Roy Stephens, managing director of Self-ridges, summed up the feelings of London's store own-ers. He said: "It is good news for us because it will bring in a lot of foreign visitors." A million extra visitors were immediately expected to pour into Britain from all over the world for the royal wedding, making it a record year for the tourist trade. An English Tourist Board spokes-man said: "You probably won't be able to get beds in London for love or money before and after the wedding day."

The souvenir trade was likely to beat the record sales during the Queen's Silver Jubilee four years ago when there was a boom in the sales of everything from tea cups to bath-towels, provided they had the royal crest or the Queen's head on them. By the afternoon of the engage-ment announcement, towels, scarves, crockery and silverware, and hundreds of other items which some shrewd businessmen had held back in warehouses hop-ing with fingers crossed that Lady Diana was the one, were being distributed throughout Britain by fleets of speeding trucks. The leading soothsayers of the stars, the astrologers, also had their share of the action. "Charles and Diana are a good love match," said one of Britain's leading experts in the field, Russell Grant. "The Prince is Scorpio and his bride-to-be Cancer. Their sun signs are as compatible as love and marriage. It's the beginning of one of the most electrifying marriages ever."

Even a computer decided that they were ideally suited. It also predicted their marriage is the one most likely to last. The analysis was made by Dateline Computer Dating – the biggest computer matchmakers in Britain. Information on Charles and his bride-to-be was fed into the computer and it returned the highest compatibility rating possible. They were said to be ideally matched on scores of interests and hobbies ranging from sports to politics and romance.

So now we know . . .

Chapter Thirteen

HOUSEKEEPING BILLS

Saving pennies to make ends meet will be one problem that Lady Diana will never have to face – after marrying one of the world's richest young men. He already receives £150,000 a year tax free and there is more to come. It will quadruple when he becomes King and begins to receive monies from the Duchy of Lancaster as well, one of the traditional property interests of a British Monarch. The Prince is also in line to inherit a fortune of up to £60 million on the death of his ailing great-aunt, the 84-year-old Duchess of Windsor. But part of the strange nature of his role is that he does not get paid, either by the nation or the Commonwealth, for being the heir apparent. He must take on extra work to raise the money, as a form of blue-blooded moonlighting.

Charles' annual salary does not cost the British taxpayer a penny. Unlike other leading members of the Royal Family, he does not receive any support through what is known as the Civil List. This is the system Parliament uses to pay the Queen and others close to her. The annual Civil List pay for other members of the Royal Family at the moment is The Queen £3,260,000 plus an estimated £500,000 from her private Duchy of Lancaster estates; Prince Philip £160,000; Princess Anne £100,000; Princess Margaret £98,000 and the Queen Mother

£286,000. Until Prince Charles was 21-years-old nearly all the income from the Duchy of Cornwall went to the British Treasury. The Queen was given £15,000 to look after the needs of her son up to the age of eighteen when she then received £30,000 from the royal lands to the west.

The total area of the Duchy is 130,000 acres, which makes Charles one of the biggest landowners in Britain. It is a mixture of farms and country homesteads, and old terraced houses, shops and at least one pub in London. Its interests are spread over Cornwall, Devon, Somerset, Dorset, Gloucestershire and Wiltshire as well as all the Isles of Scilly. There are 850 tenants in the area of Kennington in South London, and thousands more elsewhere. If Charles visits the famous Oval cricket ground in Kennington to see a Test Match, it is also a case of the landlord paying a call since he owns that green turf as well. Kennington was originally known as 'King's Town' marking the association with centuries of Dukes of Cornwall. This too belongs to the Prince. Outside London his tenants include sheep farmers on Dartmoor, Cornish tin miners, and daffodil growers in the Scillies. He also owns the notorious Dartmoor Prison. On the River Helford in Cornwall he has an oyster farm which produces a million succulent morsels every year, selling at around two and three pounds a dozen. Recently he sub-contracted this operation to a big British marketing company. Apart from having land on which hundreds of farmers are his tenants, Charles also has a 550 acre farm of his own. This is Duchy Home Farm at Stoke Climsland in East Cornwall, which breeds high quality beef cattle called Devon Red Rubies. He takes a very active interest in running the place and helps Britain's exports by selling some of his 300-strong herd to foreign breeders.

The estates, together with the title, date back to the early fourteenth century. It was Edward III who created the title in 1337 and began the tradition of passing it down through history as both an honour and source of income for the eldest sons of monarchs. Charles inherited the title when he was three-years-old, from the moment the Queen succeeded to the throne in 1952. The Dukedom, by tradition, automatically goes to a sovereign's first born male son, but only after the ruler has taken the throne. It is the oldest of such honours in nobility, because, until Edward III chose it for his six-year-old son, Edward the Black Prince, the word 'duke' did not exist in Britain. It comes from the latin 'Dux' meaning leader. King Edward's charter instituting the dukedom is still preserved in barely legible old script in the British Museum. Fortunately, for Charles today, King Edward regarded the young Prince Edward as his favourite son and showered him with castles and land under the terms of this charter. He was given the Cornish castles of Launceston, Liskeard, Restormel, Trematon and Tintagel and other castles in adjoining Devon, including the mighty fortress at Exeter. With the castles came the rights to raise an income from all the manors, villages and farms for scores of miles around the walls. Over the centuries most of the castles crumbled, but the estates prospered, expanding into a wide belt stretching to London over rich farming country and thriving towns.

The spread of the Duchy and the complexity of its affairs are enormous. Like the boss of a big business enterprise, Charles administers its affairs with the equivalent of a board of directors. To help him run what, in the 1980s, is a very up to date venture, there is an eight-strong Prince's Council. It includes some modern-day gentlemen with titles from another age, such as the Lord

Warden of the Stannaries, Keeper of the Privy Seal and Keeper of the Records. The Stannaries title comes from the latin 'stannum', meaning tin and goes back to the age when a large portion of income for the duchy was from the thriving tin mines of Cornwall. On the board are some of the best financial, legal and estate management brains in the country. His financial watchdog for example, known as the Receiver General, is youthful Mr. John Baring of Baring Brothers, the international merchant bankers based in the City of London. Keeping a day-to-day watch on the estates of the Dukedom is Mr. Anthony Gray, who, for twenty years, looked after the cash for the rich Christ Church College at Oxford University. As Secretary and Keeper of the Records he is in constant touch with the Prince, advising him and receiving instructions from him, on the running of the Duchy. Charles takes the whole business seriously, ploughing into figures, reports, plans, designs and laws on property ownership with enthusiasm. His estates are considered to be among the best run in the country.

The headquarters, with a permanent staff of twelve, is an imposing Nash-style building constructed in 1877 opposite Buckingham Palace. Such is the size of the estate that there are five sub-offices spread throughout the West Country, including a granite fortress-like mini-headquarters at St. Mary's, one of the flowery and windswept Scilly Isles. Mr. Gray, at the marble-walled headquarters, says: "The estates are not really run as profitably as they could be. The Prince tries to be a good landlord and treats his tenants fairly. What he takes out of the Duchy is not much by today's standards, when you consider that this has got to pay for his staff at Buckingham Palace, all his living expenses and cover the many donations he makes every year to charitable organisations. He is generous with his money and hardly ever ignores a request for help from an organisation within the Duchy. He gives away an incredible amount of his income."

The total value of the Duchy has never been properly assessed. The total income of the Duchy for 1980 totalled more than £32 million, most of this coming from rents. But commercial rents are not charged. At Kennington, for example, rents are deliberately kept low to help the mainly elderly and poorly paid who live in the district. A visit from the landlord is not usually welcome by most people, but when Charles visits his tenants he is greeted with loud cheers. The streets were decorated for him when he last wandered round his Kennington property. Among those he met living there were his former nanny, Miss Helen Lightbody, and a dozen or more other ex-royal servants. He popped into one of the local pubs, the Sir Sydney Smith, where landlord Alfie Goff offered to pull him a pint, but Charles declined – "I've had my fair share today, thank you." Charles has a home next door to the regional headquarters of the Duchy at St. Mary's in the Scillies. It's on the very tip of England pointing across the Atlantic from the English Channel. This secluded hideaway, the cottage called Tamarisk, is alongside the offices of the estate. It even has an old cannon on the lawns, put there in the sixteenth century to fight off Spanish invaders.

In accordance with the age of the title, Charles receives a handful of strange feudal dues, apart from the cash, as master of the Duchy. Among the odd 'rents' are: a load of firewood, a grey cloak, 100 old shillings, a pound of pepper, a hunting bow, gilt spurs, a pound of herbs, a salmon spear, a pair of leather gloves and two greyhounds. These exotic offerings were handed over to the Black Prince when he used to ride down to the West Country for drinking, wenching and hunting with his medieval friends. Six hundred years later the current duke is still entitled to them, though armour-clad knights no longer hammer on the doors of the poor peasantry for these gifts. He last received such tributes in a much less rousing manner in 1973, amid the ruins of Launceston's Norman castle. Instead of frightened mobs fearful of more demands being made upon them by the royal gentry, there were thousands of happy tenants, watching a formal ceremony in which representatives of the various manors of the Duchy delivered their strange presents.

Chapter Fourteen

KING IN WAITING

Although Diana will have to bow completely to the wishes of her future in-laws, she will, unlike most other brides, have no worries about the years ahead. A marriage bureau would describe the man she is marrying as having excellent prospects, to say the least. What sort of future will Diana and Charles have as a King and Queen in waiting? When Charles was about to graduate from Cambridge, he was given a booklet called 'Choosing a Career'. His fellow students may have found it useful, but he had no need of it. The Prince's future has never been in doubt, and he has been prepared for his destiny. He is almost ready to be a king, and more than competent to cope with the responsibilities of the monarchy.

The King-to-be has been carefully groomed for the part, but unlike an actor, he does not know when he will have to go on stage to play the role. The date of the 'opening night' is still unknown. There has been much speculation, though, about the possibility of the Queen abdicating early, to make way for Prince Charles while he is still young. The throne did not come to Queen Victoria's eldest son, Edward Prince of Wales, until he was sixty. He became bored with waiting and turned to a dissolute life among shady friends and mistresses. Whilst Charles does not share any characteristics with

Edward VII, it would be a pity, some argue, if he had to wait too long before his coronation. The Queen, happily, is still a healthy woman, content with her job, and as deeply interested as ever in the affairs of State. The constant travel and public engagements of the Silver Jubilee celebrations proved arduous for her occasionally, but that was an exceptional year.

Charles has dismissed suggestions that his mother should soon give up the throne in his favour. He sees no reason why she should retire. He feels that, because of the vast constitutional and political knowledge a monarch acquires by the time he or she reaches normal retirement age, the sovereign is then at a "most useful stage". If the Queen lives to the ages of her mother, grandmother, or great-great-grandmother Queen Victoria – eighty-two – it could be the beginning of the twenty-first century before Charles reaches the throne. No wonder he has forecast that it might be as long as forty years before he is crowned, though one does not know how seriously he takes this proposition. Yet his growing involvement with royal duties and an indicator of his future was so dramatically demonstrated four years ago.

It was like a scene from a fairy tale, a Queen in a golden coach pulled by six white horses and a handsome Prince in a dashing uniform riding behind her in triumphal procession among cheering masses. This happened in London on the memorable 7 June, 1977, as part of the Silver Jubilee celebrations marking the twenty-fifth anniversary of the Queen's accession to the throne.

The Queen, with the Duke of Edinburgh sitting alongside her, waved to the crowds through the windows of the 216-year-old Golden State Coach. Riding in a place of honour just behind the right wheel was Prince Charles.

The Prince was mounted on a sleek black horse just given to him by the Mounties. With a silver sword at his side, he was dressed in the tall bearskin and crimson jacket of a colonel in the Welsh Guards. Across his chest was a lavish display of decorations. In truth, a suitable escort for a Queen. That he was posted in pride of place near to his parents, signified the ever-increasing official role he now has in royal life. He is gradually taking from his parents much of the burden of public appearances and world tours. He is getting more deeply involved in the responsibility of preserving the crown and running the nation.

Preserving the Commonwealth is also one of Charles' great aims in life. He likes to think there is a family spirit about it, where everyone feels they know each other, that they have something in common. These come about, he believes, from a common language, common culture, common experience and common history. He has pointed out on more than one occasion that the Queen is no longer just the Queen of England. Thanks to several Acts of Parliament in Australia, Canada and New Zealand, she is also just as much "owned" as their Queen by these nations as she is the Queen of Great Britain. This was the point he tried to make when he gave a confusing answer to a question during the July 1977 Commonwealth Youth Conference. In an off-the-cuff reply he said: "I don't think it would be a disaster if Britain withdrew from the Commonwealth and I am sure it could survive without Britain." He was saying this to try to show the strength of the Commonwealth as he sees it. He also said: "I believe that the Queen, as head of the Commonwealth, is an important part of keeping the whole thing together." Two hundred young Commonwealth delegates who gathered in London, from forty-five countries, were given a clear indication too about how Charles pins his hopes on them: "Above all I believe it is up to the young of the Commonwealth to show that they believe that association has something to offer the modern world, because without your support, interest and encouragement, it will only be a matter of time before the whole thing fades away through lack of interest."

Charles sees his task as one who can break the differences of colour, racialism, political systems, languages, richness and poverty, to keep together what is still one of the liveliest international alliances in the world. He is also helping to keep the Commonwealth idea of unity alive, showing how the throne can still act as the imperial lynch-pin. This is especially important at a time when there is talk of cutting ties with Britain in Australia and calls for separatism in Canada.

Charles has been trained for kingship in a period when society is becoming more egalitarian. The monarchy has been forced to keep in step with the developments in the streets outside palaces and castles. Charles revealed his awareness of the new society when he said: "In these times the monarchy is called into question – it is not taken for granted as it used to be. In that sense one has to be far more professional, I think, than one ever used to be." Of the task ahead, he once said: "I've been trained to do it and I feel part of the job. I have this feeling of duty towards England, towards the United Kingdom and the Commonwealth. I feel there is a great deal I can do if I am given the chance to do it."

In the next few years he may join the Diplomatic Service, perhaps doing a job linked with exporting British goods. An appointment as a Governor General of a Commonwealth country could happen now he has a bride and would give him and his wife two or three years of running a 'junior court' before returning to Britain, and a possible coronation. The only trade Charles has been prepared for is that of kingship. His grandfather, George VI, once said: "We're not a family, we're a firm." Already he is a 'junior director' of the enterprise, but unlike most bosses' sons, he cannot easily leave the family business. His role is pre-ordained, unless he wants to cause a constitutional crisis like his late great uncle, the Duke of Windsor, and abdicate. He will take his throne at a time of changing attitudes toward monarchies. He realises that the days of the aloof king on a golden throne are over, and that the continuation of his own inheritance is being questioned in the Houses of Parliament.

With this in mind he has tried, probably harder than any of his predecessors, to get close to the people he will rule one day. He wants to know how people live and cope in changing societies, what they are thinking – their ambitions, their hates and their loves. He once admitted he had no idea how people existed in small houses or rented flats, or how they coped on meagre salaries. His understanding is growing because he has constantly sought to meet as many people as possible from all walks of life to learn how they hope to fulfil their ambitions. Prince Charles says frankly: "I'm not a normal person in the sense that I was born to be king. I have received a special education and training. I could never be a normal person because I have been prepared to reign over my subjects." His popularity at home and abroad shows that he is succeeding in breaking down the barriers between palace and people.

Whatever he does before his coronation, he is a well-equipped heir. No king in British history has made so great an effort to get to know as many of his future subjects, to learn so much about the countries he will rule and explore so many different parts of the world. When the Prince takes his throne with his Queen alongside him, it will more than likely be as King Charles III, but if he wishes he could choose another name. A monarch is not restricted to the names with which he was baptised. Even if he sticks to his four Christian names he could also be known as King Philip, King Arthur or King George VII. Whatever kingly name he picks it is to be hoped that he fares better than the previous rules named Charles. Charles I was beheaded in front of the Banqueting Hall in Whitehall one winter's day in 1649, while Charles II, the pleasure-loving 'Merry Monarch', is reputed to have died from mercury poisoning in 1685. He had a fatal tendency to meddle in the wonders of chemistry.

The line of succession to the throne after Charles is: Prince Andrew, Prince Edward, Princess Anne and her offspring, Princess Margaret and her children, Viscount Linley and Lady Sarah Armstrong-Jones, the Duke of Gloucester, Prince William of Gloucester and the Duke of Kent. A youthful king would be popular both at home and abroad. The Queen was only twenty-six when she came to the throne and there were hopes of a new expanding Elizabethan Age for Britain. For many reasons that feeling of a national renaissance slowly died away amid a shattered economy and disintegrating colonial outposts. Could a young leader like Charles, with his tremendous energy, put vitality and purpose back into the country again? Rekindle the spirit that his mother generated in her day? Provide a new unifying force for the Commonwealth?

While waiting, Charles feels that he can still contribute something useful to the life of the monarchy and the country, such as the work he did towards the organising of his mother's Jubilee Year, or his active interest in young people's problems and the efforts he makes on behalf of Wales. Since leaving the Royal Navy, Charles has taken the trouble to study in greater detail the constitutional role of the Crown, though he believes real knowledge of what a king can and cannot do comes from experience. "You learn the way a monkey learns, watching its parents," he once told the *Observer*. He has trained for kingship in a period when society has become more egalitarian. The age of the common man.

Charles feels that the Palace is keeping pace, however, with the times, and the Royal Family is changing its life-style. Pointing this out, when addressing the New South Wales Parliament in Sidney, he remarked that it was not always easy to do this: "It is more difficult to adapt when the accepted patterns of life and society change so unusually fast." He thought however, that because the monarchy was adapting to new conditions, the institution had become the strongest support of a stable Government in Britain.

Chapter Fifteen

QUEEN IN WAITING

Diana's second day as the future Princess of Wales must have been quite a shock to a teenager used to complete freedom, giving her a quick foretaste of the way the rest of her life would be mapped out now both as a princess and one day as Queen. She woke in what was to be her new home for the next few months of her engagement, the spare bedroom in Clarence House. Outside she could hear the sound of hob-nailed boots ringing on the cobblestones as a soldier wearing a furry bearskin helmet and scarlet jacket, his rifle sloped on his shoulder, paced backwards and forwards in front of the house's black wooden gates. On the other side of the house one of the special squad of uniformed Metropolitan policemen guarding the Queen Mother was on duty sitting in a small green hut. A uniformed footman brought Lady Diana tea on a silver salver. The teenager was more used to getting up and making instant coffee for herself in the kitchen of her flat. Later, the Prince of Wales' lady brought a touch of teenage style to the Royal household by coming down to breakfast with the Queen Mother dressed in a pair of her favourite jeans and a sweater. Not that the eighty-year-old Queen Mother noticed, for she was used to having teenagers round the house. Her grandchildren Viscount Linley and Lady Sarah

Armstrong-Jones, Princess Margaret's children, often stayed in Clarence House.

Diana felt completely at ease in the company of her Royal breakfast companion. The Queen Mother had been a frequent guest during Diana's childhood and had often watched her play with her other grandchildren, Prince Andrew and Prince Edward. Another breakfast guest made it an even more relaxed atmosphere, Ruth, Lady Fermoy, the Queen Mother's Lady-in-Waiting and Diana's grandmother. Over the next few months as the regal Queen Mother began to share a lifetime's experience of public service with Diana, preparing the teenager for the role she will have to play in society, the rest of the Royal Family would begin to spot the similarities between the girl Prince Charles picked for his bride and his much-loved granny.

Both are sweet natured but strong, and both are the youngest daughters of earls and have instant rapport with children, wild animals and press photographers. Over the difficult six months of her courtship, constantly pestered by cameramen, Diana remained patient, cool and polite. While Charles and even the Queen lost their temper with the constant attention, Diana alone remained calm. On the Queen Mother's eightieth birthday in 1980, Fleet Street photographers, normally the most cynical of men, spent their beer money on a beautiful china bowl and huge bunch of flowers for their favourite Royal camera subject. All through her long years of public service the Queen Mother has always made sure that the cameramen got their pictures. None of the other Royals, including Prince Charles, would ever bother that much. The Fleet Street men adore her and have started to like Lady Diana in the same way, especially as on the evening after the engagement announcement she had especially turned to give them a wave and a first class news picture as she made her way to Clarence House.

On this, her second day as a prospective Royal Lady, Diana did not disappoint the photographers either. She had even begun to develop her own kind of regal wave, and her head was held proud, no longer the shy girl who was photographed so often on the pavement outside Coleherne Court. It was to her old flat she was driven this morning, her new detective by her side, to visit her beloved home for the last time. In the rush of engagement day she had forgotten a few necessities. But she only stayed there for five minutes, emerging with a brown leather holdall before driving to Buckingham Palace for lunch with the Queen. For Prince Charles, meanwhile, life went on as usual. He was up at dawn, driving in his green Range Rover, dressed in a green tweed jacket, off to see a new possible racehorse to replace the deceased Allibar. Diana didn't see her fiancé that night, as he was in Hampshire on one of his fixed engagements, dining with officers of the 2nd King Edward VIII's Own Gurkha Rifles as their Colonel-in-Chief. The couple wouldn't meet again for the next two days as the Prince carried out his diary of engagements.

Late on Wednesday night the Prince flew to Scotland to prepare for his tour of a Clyde coastguard station the next day. On Thursday, as Diana was preparing to meet her mother, who had flown in from Australia, the Prince was in Greenock getting kissed by a pretty girl. Throughout his years as a bachelor Prince, the game of kissing Charles had become a regular feature of his duties. Wherever he seemed to go, in whatever part of the world – Australia, America, South America and even just recently in India – there always seemed to be a pretty girl on hand who wanted to kiss him. This time it was Anne Winton, aged nineteen, who at least had the good manners to ask first. Most Royal kissers just kissed first and asked questions later. The Scottish housewives packing the pavements outside the coastguard base shouted "She's a lovely lass", and the Prince, wiping away the lipstick, beamed with delight.

Mrs. Frances Shand-Kydd arrived at Heathrow from a Qantas flight and revealed she was one of the first to know the good news. "I am a very proud mother," she said. She marched briskly through a crowd of pressmen and when one photographer commented on her speed she said, "I've got good long legs like my daughter." That evening mother and daughter met at a secret rendezvous for dinner; they had a lot to talk about.

Diana and Charles were together that week-end, staying with friends in Cheshire and holding hands they went to Sunday morning Church service; there was no need to hide anymore. Over the next four weeks the couple snatched as much time together as the Prince's diary would allow, for they knew they faced yet another long, lonely separation. That week-end Buckingham Palace released details of yet another long foreign tour for the Prince, this time to the other side of the world. Charles was to fly off on 29 March to Wellington, New Zealand at the start of a six week tour which would take him to Australia, Venezuela and the United States of America. The Prince had long been tipped as the next Governor General of Australia and the British Press saw this trip as a lead in to an announcement of his new job. At that stage there were no plans for Diana to fly with him in his RAF VC10, but there were plans for Diana to join the Prince in Washington at the end of the tour when he had been invited to dine with President Ronald Reagan on 2 May. After that date the Prince's red leather official diary was empty for two weeks. Plans were made for the young couple to holiday together somewhere in the Caribbean, an island paradise where they could find some peace and quiet before the rush of the great day in July.

On 3 March, they named the day – 29 July, and the place – St. Paul's Cathedral in the City of London. It was the future Princess of Wales who picked St. Paul's, simply because it's bigger. St. Paul's can hold several hundred more guests than the more usual Royal marriage spot, Westminster Abbey, and it was Lady Diana herself who suggested the Cathedral so that as many people as possible could be invited. But perhaps, in the back of Diana's mind was the thought that her mother's own unsuccessful marriage began at Westminster Abbey and she did not want to walk down the same aisle. It was a Royal first for St. Paul's, the first Royal Marriage ever to be held there. The immense task of planning for that day began immediately. Millions of people would flood into the capital for the ceremonial carriage procession from Buckingham Palace to the Cathedral. At the beginning of 1981 the Duke of Norfolk, aged 65, had been warned by Buckingham Palace to keep his official engagement diary free from mid-April to 31 July.

The wedding at which the new Archbishop of Canterbury, Dr. Robert Runcie would officiate, would be a completely new experience for the staff of St. Paul's. The rest of the Royal Family, the Queen and Prince Philip, the Queen Mother, Princess Anne and Princess Margaret were all married at Westminster Abbey. The Rev. Alan Webster, Dean of St. Paul's, called an urgent meeting with the Cathedral surveyor and members of his works staff immediately he was told the news in a special letter delivered by an envoy from the Queen's Private Secretary. The Cathedral is capable of holding at least 2,000 people and BBC and ITV would beam the ceremony and the procession to 500 million people throughout the world, even behind the Iron Curtain.

Lady Diana and the Prince would take a prime role in the planning of their big day. Diana's most important jobs would be to supervise the guest list and to choose the wedding gown. She hinted to friends that she was looking at designs in pure silk and chiffon with a touch of antique lace. The Queen went to the House of Hartnell for her jewel and pearl encrusted wedding dress in November 1947 and Diana's mother also wore a Hartnell creation for her own wedding in June 1954. Lady Diana's wedding ring will be made from Welsh gold, of course. Could the new Princess of Wales wear anything else? The Queen, the Queen Mother, Princess Anne and Princess Margaret all have wedding rings made from a nugget mined in Wales in 1923. The day before the engagement announcement Diana was seen shopping for romantic nightwear at that top people's lingerie boutique, the Janet Reger Shop in Knightsbridge. The shop sells pure silk nightgowns at £100 a time. What she bought must remain a secret between her, the boudoir and Prince Charles.

Honeymoon plans gave some headache to Buckingham Palace and the young couple themselves. Where do Royal newly-weds go to get away from the world to be alone at last? What chance would they have with the world's press trailing them every last inch of the way? When young Princess Elizabeth married her handsome sailor Philip in October 1947 the couple tried to have a quiet honeymoon at Broadlands, the Estate of the

Mountbattens in Romsey, Hampshire. But hundreds of sightseers stormed the estate to try to see the couple and they were forced to move to Scotland for some peace and quiet. The Royal Yacht *Britannia* was used by Princess Margaret and Tony Armstrong-Jones in 1960 and by Princess Anne and Captain Mark Phillips in November 1973 for Caribbean honeymoon cruises. The privacy of the Royal Yacht would be a good choice; so too would be the hideaways used by the Prince over his bachelor years. The couple seem determined to keep their honeymoon destination a complete secret but the best bet does seem the Royal Yacht in the Caribbean with a stop off possibly at the island of Nevis in the Bahamas. A romantic cottage with a four-poster bed looking out on to a palm-fringed beach was checked out by Scotland Yard security men at the beginning of February.

Meanwhile in the run up to her wedding, Lady Diana went to evening classes to take her first lessons on how to behave as a member of the Royal family. Her teacher for the future Princess of Wales' first official engagement was of course her fiancé Prince Charles. The job he picked for her entry into public life was an easy one . . . a recital in aid of the Royal Opera House Development Appeal at Goldsmith's Hall in the City of London on Monday evening, 9 March. The engagement had been in the Prince's diary since before Christmas and was chosen because Lady Diana and Charles both share a love of the opera. This was the moment when international royal protocol decreed that the prince's nineteen-year-old fiancée should be kept firmly in her place. While Charles was allowed to plant a kiss on the cheek of Her Serene Highness, the Princess of Monaco, Diana was obliged to dip in a curtsey to this wife of a head of state.

The fact that she had to do this to a former film star

emphasised the fact that she will have to curtsey to many of the other royals of Europe until the day of her wedding when she becomes Princess of Wales. From then on the role she will play on international royal life will be very different and Princess Grace and other European princesses will be her equal. Kisses on the cheek will become the order of the day when Diana meets other royals, and many of the members of the more junior royal houses will have to curtsey to Lady Diana after her marriage. In order of precedence she will be third in line after the Queen and the Queen Mother because of her new role as wife of the heir to the British throne. Until then, as the daughter of an earl, there are thirty-eight categories of women who officially are senior to her in public in England (in Scotland there are 20 senior to her).

Diana discovered the next day at the breakfast table with the Queen Mother that her plunge into public life had amazed millions. Perhaps the young lady did not realise how much of her creamy white skin she was revealing to the world by wearing an amazing black silk creation. Her dress became that day the second biggest talking point in Britain . . . the first was a savage Government budget which put up everything from petrol to drink and cigarettes . . . to the British public Lady Diana's cleavage provided a little light relief from the price rises. The Buckingham Palace switchboard was flooded with calls from the public.

Lady Diana had gone to the Brook Street, Mayfair, salon run by Elizabeth and David Emanuel the previous week after Prince Charles told her what her first public engagement was to be. She told the designers that she was going to a very glamorous evening where one of the guests was to be Princess Grace of Monaco. "I'll leave the choice of style up to you," she told the Emanuels.

The stunning black dress was made from silk taffeta with a fitted bodice and full skirt over a stiffened petticoat. The bodice which was dotted with black sequins and the dress came with a matching black cape. Elizabeth and David Emanuel, married and still in their twenties with two young children insisted, "Diana loved it. The dress was very tasteful exactly the right dress for the occasion. There is no way it could be called rude." Diana was said to be delighted by the effect, so delighted that she picked the virtually unknown David and Elizabeth to make her wedding dress in preference to all the established Royal dress designers, like the House of Hartnell and Ian Thomas. David and Elizabeth, who greet their clients, even the Royal ones, casually dressed in jeans and sweaters, just couldn't believe their luck. "We will make her into a fairy tale princess for her wedding day with a glamorous gown which will amaze everyone."

The young bride-to-be will find herself cut off from her own family much more than other wives. This is because the Royal Family is such a close-knit unit, constantly supporting one another in their unique position in life. Her new husband is particularly fond of life at home with his nearest and dearest – a habit Lady Diana may wish to break after a few years if she is going to establish her own home as an independent stronghold of junior Royals. Some of Charles' happiest moments are when he is with his family, whose sense of unity provides a welcome relief from the pressures around it. When Charles is abroad he is in constant touch with his mother and father, brothers and sisters or grandmother and aunt, either by telephone or by letter. No member of the group does anything without discussing it first with the others and hardly any commitment is made without family approval.

154

The Queen, who succeeded to the throne when Charles was three-years-and-three-months-old, had also been brought up in a warm family circle. The Victorian habit of banning the children to the nursery and rarely seeing them until they could either shoot or ride, had long since died by the time of her own childhood. Because of the loving atmosphere she remembered with her parents, she arranged that there would be no barriers of governesses and nannies between herself and her own children. Now that Charles is getting married and Princess Anne has a family life of her own, the Queen sees less of her eldest children, though the Prince tries to be with his mother and father as often as he can. Every morning when he is in London he begins his day by leaving his own rooms at the front of Buckingham Palace to join his parents for breakfast in their quarters at the rear of the building. His mother's day usually starts at eight o'clock in the morning, listening to the radio and reading the morning papers and personal letters. Breakfast is at nine o'clock with Prince Philip and the rest of the family. In the Palace grounds below the window, a bagpiper often plays a few cheerful tunes to get the morning moving. Until lunchtime the Queen concentrates on reading State papers, dealing with official correspondence, and discussing the running of the household with her staff. She holds audiences at noon and after a light lunch she leaves for afternoon engagements. At five o'clock in the afternoon she feeds her corgis – distributing the food into several bowls with a silver fork and spoon. If neither she nor Philip have any evening engagements, they often eat a simple supper on a tray, watching television comedy shows. This will be the sort of life-style that the new Princess of Wales will have to get used to when she and her husband are carrying out royal duties from Buckingham Palace.

It will be an odd world for Diana to bring up her children in. She will lose, in time, virtually all her friends from her free teenage years. She will not be able to take the risk of someone talking: no one in the Royal Family laughs off a breach of etiquette. Diana will not be able to use her husband's first name in public and she will not be able to travel anywhere without prior arrangements and a detective beside her. She will have wealth and position, but at what cost? She will be expected to go with the Prince on the many hundreds of engagements he carries out each year from visiting shopping centres, and exhibitions, to planting trees. But she is likely to be spared military inspections and regimental dinners. She will accompany the Prince on the two or three foreign tours he makes each year. Every moment of her time will be taken up with receptions, private meetings, walks around schools, universities and factories. Her every move will be timed to the last detail. Guards of honour will greet her at every foreign airport or quayside. Guest lists will be checked most carefully and everything down to who enters what room first will be set out for her by an ever-present entourage. Diana will, of course, live largely at public expense, never having to wash her own dishes, something she always did in Coleherne Court, never worrying about a mortgage or paying for her children's education and eventually when she becomes Queen, she will have a choice of seven beautiful buildings to call home.

In the parade ring at Sandown Park racecourse on what was to be an unlucky Friday, 13 March for her fiancé, Diana was really starting to look the part as a future member of the Royal Family. The Prince was riding in the 3.25 on his new mount, Good Prospect, and Diana, flanked by the Queen Mother and Princess Margaret went to see him saddle up for the three miles Grand Military Gold Cup. Diana chatted with all the racecourse officials and other jockeys like a real Royal trouper where the rule is . . . a quick word with everyone. Occasionally the Queen Mother would give her a comforting touch on the arm as if to reassure her that everything was going fine. It can't have been a pleasant experience for a teenager with everyone staring at her as if she were a well bred racehorse herself, but she carried it off well. Her composure broke temporarily when the Prince took a nosedive at the eighteenth fence. She half stood up in the Royal Box and then put her head down, obviously too frightened to look in case her fiancé was hurt. She stayed that way until a tap on the shoulder from Princess Margaret assured her that all was well. Charles meanwhile was picking himself up, apparently unhurt except for a bruised and bleeding nose. In the unsaddling enclosure Diana was waiting to greet him with a hug and an anxious "Are you all right?" As 'Action Man's' wife she will have to get used to a touch of nerves as her husband continues his daredevil antics.

Diana will soon be known as Her Royal Highness and she will have to act like one. For the rest of her life this quiet girl will have to cope with her every public smile being recorded, her clothes copied and her behaviour studied. Her life from now on will never be entirely her own. She must have sensed something of the loneliness she will face under guard in palaces and stately homes because she asked her flatmates to keep in touch. Leaving them her new private phone number at Clarence House she begged, "For God's sake ring me up. I'm going to need you."